Studio Art Quilt Associates, Inc.

# Portfolio 16

*The art quilt sourcebook*

Edited by Cheryl Dineen Ferrin

**Studio Art Quilt Associates**

P.O. Box 572
Storrs, CT 06268-0572
860-487-4199
www.SAQA.com • info@SAQA.com

Front cover (clockwise):
Patty Hawkins, *Aspen Solace 2*
Sue Benner, *Body Parts (Zebra Sleeve, Paisley Sleeve)*
Mary-Ellen Latino, *Undulations VI: Grace*

Back cover (clockwise):
Jean Neblett, *Reflections 22: Sharon Woods In Winter*
Virginia Abrams, *A Swimmer's Vision of the Lake*
Kathleen Sharp, *Goat in a Boat*

Title page:
Jae McDonald, *Spring*

Above:
Carol Watkins, *Prairie Rainbow*

Page 295:
Tove Pirajá Hansen, *New Beginnings: hope, light, life and will*

*Studio Art Quilt Associates, Inc. Portfolio 16*
*The Art Quilt Sourcebook*
Published by Studio Art Quilt Associates, Inc.
All rights reserved.
Copyright © 2009 by Studio Art Quilt Associates, Inc.
Editor: Cheryl Dineen Ferrin
Book Design & Production: C. Dineen Ferrin Designs
Cover Design: Deidre Adams

ISBN-13: 978-0-9788853-3-5
ISBN-10: 0-9788853-3-3

Printed in China

Studio Art Quilt Associates, Inc.
P.O. Box 572, Storrs, Connecticut 06268-0572 USA
860-487-4199
www.SAQA.com ● info@SAQA.com

Studio Art Quilt Associates, Inc. is supported by generous donations from individuals and organizations, including our Platinum Sponsors:

INTERNATIONAL QUILT FESTIVAL
35 YEARS · 1974-2009 · HOUSTON

American Quilter's Society
www.americanquilter.com

J. T. TRADING
CORPORATION
Distributor of
5 5 SPRAY AND FIX

website: www.sprayandfix.com
Telephone: 860-350-5565

and these other fine businesses:

Silver Sponsor:
　　AmericanStyle Magazine

Corporate Sponsors:
　　Fairfield Processing Corporation
　　Global Interprint
　　Mountain Mist
　　Professional Quilter Magazine
　　Quilt Surface Design Symposium
　　Quilter's Newsletter Magazine
　　Selvedge Magazine
　　Surface Design Association

SAQA Lecture Series Sponsors:
　　C&T Publishing
　　Empty Spools Seminars
　　Meander Publishing

Sponsored by

Over 20,000 Fabrics Online and In Stock

# Introduct

Now in its twentieth year, Studio Art Quilt Associates, Inc. brings you another new and exciting collection of original fiber art quilts. *Portfolio 16* offers you glimpses of some of the latest works from 285 professional artists in 17 countries, including a tremendous selection of work from artists in the U.S. and Canada.

SAQA defines an art quilt as *a contemporary artwork exploring and expressing aesthetic concerns common to the whole range of visual arts, which retains, through materials or technique, a clear relationship to the folk art quilt from which it descends*. Each of the artists included in *Portfolio 16* is a professional artist member of SAQA and interprets this definition in their own way; they are known for pushing the boundaries of the medium and exploring new territory. Come visit our Web site at www.SAQA.com and the on-line gallery from time to time to see even more great images

of fiber art quilts. Our executive director, Martha Sielman, would be happy to provide further information about art quilts and becoming a member or sponsor of SAQA. Contact Ms. Sielman at 860-487-4199 or e-mail her at: info@SAQA.com.

Studio Art Quilt Associates, Inc. is a non-profit organization whose mission is to promote the art quilt through education, exhibitions, professional development and documentation. Founded in 1989 by an initial group of 50 artists, SAQA members now number over 2,400: artists, teachers, collectors, gallery owners, museum curators and corporate sponsors.

Whether you are a collector, curator or critic, we encourage you to use this Portfolio as a reference for your work in the arts. Immerse yourself in page after page and see the tactile, technological and traditional merge to create some of the most innovative art works being produced today. Let's get started by viewing some of the stunning works in the John M. Walsh III collection and reading about what inspires him to collect these unique and visionary works of fiber art.

Judith Content, *Prism*
Collection John M. Walsh III

M. Joan Lintault, *In the Grass*
Collection John M. Walsh III

# Collector Profile: John M. Walsh III

By Sandra Sider, SAQA Vice President

John M. Walsh III ("Jack") began purchasing studio quilts in 1992, after viewing a BBC program in which Michael James discussed his work. Today the Walsh Collection numbers 82 quilts, many on the theme of water, and continues to grow at the rate of four or five quilts per year. Thirty percent of the artists in his collection are Professional Artist Members of SAQA, including Valerie Goodwin and Terrie Hancock Mangat, who are currently working on commissions for the Walsh Collection.

Approximately ten percent of the 82 quilts have been commissioned by Walsh, who has been advised from the beginning of his collecting by quilt expert Penny McMorris. Walsh says that working with McMorris has been a "collaborative effort—in large measure, my collection is a result of her vision." Walsh plans to continue to focus on commissions, which help fulfill the purposes of his collection:

• To preserve the vitality and creativity of this medium as it continues to grow and achieve new dimensions

• To nourish this work by supporting the artists, and occasionally to provide the opportunity for individual artists to pursue their vision, free from economic pressures, and to gain visibility for their work

Content two years ago about making a quilt for the collection, she immediately thought of waterfalls. Her quilt *Prism* "was inspired by memories of shimmering rainbows created when water is laced by light." Content had a very positive experience working with Walsh: "[It was] completely different from any commission I had previously experienced. Unlike most corporate and residential commissions, Jack afforded complete freedom in terms of size, color, composition. There were no parameters except that the commission must be large (no problem) and had to deal with water in some form or other. And after all, Jack wrote [to] me, water is ice, fog, mist...all of which are consistent sources of inspiration for my work."

Valerie Goodwin has expanded her creative focus while working on a commission for the collector: "The quilt that I am currently creating for Jack Walsh has been very liberating. He is an experienced patron of the arts and he lets the artist assume control of the design vision. I have thoroughly enjoyed the whole process. It gave me the opportunity to

Because water purification has been a key element of Walsh's professional life, his commissioned quilts are related in some way to water or nature. This focus began 14 years ago when he commissioned British artist Pauline Burbidge to create a water-related quilt, for which she interpreted reflections on a local river. That commission encouraged her to explore this type of imagery, resulting in several remarkable quilts on the same subject. When Walsh contacted Judith

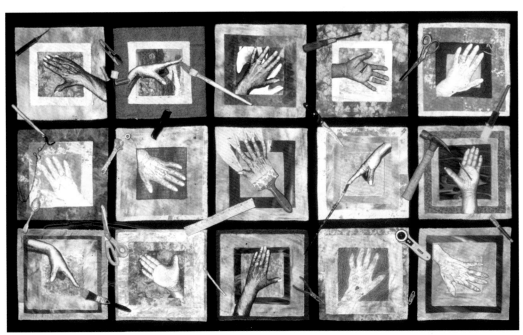

BJ Adams, *Hand Tools*, Collection John M. Walsh III

# *Collector Profile:* John M. Walsh III (continued)

explore some ideas about composition that I have been interested in as an architect. This has been the opportunity of a lifetime!" For her Walsh commission, Sue Benner was able to explore "water as both surface and depth, and how these ideas can be represented in fabric." Walsh encouraged Benner "to be ambitious" as she commenced her project, and to take all the time she needed.

In 2009, the San Jose Museum of Quilts and Textiles featured 29 quilts from the Walsh collection in *Reservoir: John M. Walsh III Collects. This was* the first time that his quilts inspired by water and nature were showcased in a major exhibition. Deborah Corsini, the museum's curator, discussed Walsh's approach to commissions in the gallery guide: "The only requirement is that he wants the quilt to be large in scale to engage and push the envelope of artistic creativity. He allows artists time to develop and create their work, often a luxury when doing a commission.... Some artists share the process and progress of their commissions, but Walsh is careful not to get in the way of the creativity and avoids creative suggestions."

For this quilt enthusiast, commissions are a "very enriching aspect of the whole collecting experience." His artists would certainly agree.

For more information, see Robert Shaw's essay "John M. Walsh III: Passionate Patron of the Quilt," at www.saqa.com/news/WalshCollection.aspx. Also, Valerie Goodwin discusses the progress of her Walsh commission at www.quiltsbyvalerie.blogspot.com.

Sue Benner, *Wisconsin Wetlands II: River Bend*
Collection John M. Walsh III

Robin Schwalb, *Chinese Characters*, Collection John M. Walsh III

# Linda Abrams

On The Edge Of Self Discovery
© 2007
43" x 51"
109 x 130 cm

21 Robbins Lane
Lake Success, New York  11020  USA
516-829-3859
info@lindasartisticadventures.com
www.lindasartisticadventures.com

# Virginia Abrams

Photo: Carson Zullinger

555 Holly Knoll Road
Hockessin, Delaware  19707  USA
302-239-5110
ginnyabrams@msn.com
www.VirginiaAbrams.com

A Swimmer's Vision of the Lake
© 2008
52" x 71"
132 x 180 cm

# B.J. Adams

Photo: PRS Associates

Variations on 'V' (Vines)
© 2007
29" x 16"
74 x 41 cm

2821 Arizona Terrace, N.W.
Washington, D.C.  20016  USA
202-364-8404
bjfiber@aol.com
www.BJAdamsArt.com

# Deidre Adams

P.O. Box 631001  |  Composition VIII
Littleton, Colorado  80163  USA  |  © 2008
303-683-0316  |  39" x 39"
deidre@deidreadams.com  |  99 x 99 cm
www.deidreadams.com

# Natalya Aikens

Piterskoie Okno/St. Pete Window 16
© 2009
9" x 9"
23 x 23 cm

69 Ridgeview Drive
Pleasantville, New York 10570 USA
917-414-7969
natalya@artbynatalya.com
www.artbynatalya.com

# Katherine K. Allen

Photo: Gerhard Heidersberger

707 S.W. 14 Court
Fort Lauderdale, Florida 33315 USA
954-253-5224
softart@mac.com
www.KatherineKAllen.com

Night Song
© 2009
22" x 13"
56 x 33 cm

# Mary Andrews

Sand Dollar #11
© 2007
24" x 20"
61 x 51 cm

423 Lockmoor Court
Grand Blanc, Michigan  48439  USA
810-695-0583
mary@maryandrewsartquilts.com
www.maryandrewsartquilts.com

# Britta Ankenbauer

Photo: Jens Stolinski

Siedlerweg 10
D-04158 Leipzig
Germany
0049 (0)341-2465216
britta@ankenbauer.com
www.britta-ankenbauer.de

Lesenacht (Night in the Library)
© 2009
32" x 40"
80 x 102 cm

# Ilse Anysas-Salkauskas

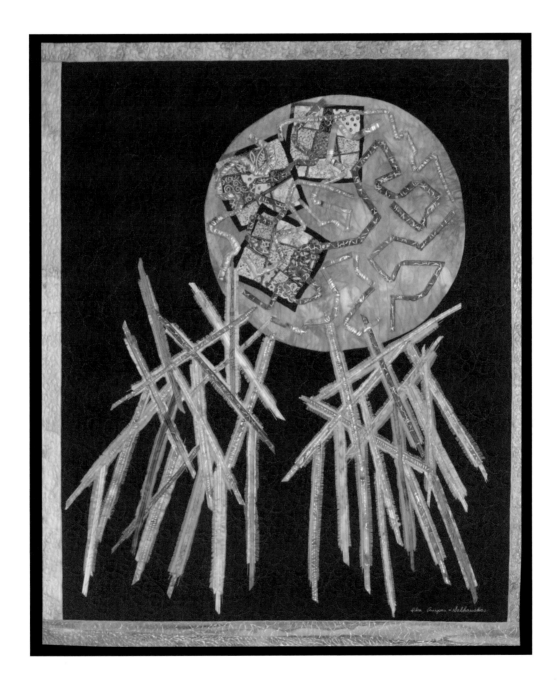

Must We Bear Crosses
© 2008
39" x 31"
99 x 79 cm

P.O. Box 93
Cochrane, Alberta  T4C 1A4
Canada
403-932-2285
ilse@anm.org
www.ilse.anm.org

# Ludmila Aristova

Photo: D. James Dee

8020 4th Avenue #A6
Brooklyn, New York  11209  USA
718-745-2597 • Fax: 212-925-5695
Ludmila.Aristova@mac.com
www.ludmilaaristova.com

Nostalgia
© 2007
26" x 35"
66 x 89 cm

# Jill Ault

Of Lake Huron
© 2008
34" x 47"
86 x 119 cm

2531 Meade Court
Ann Arbor, Michigan 48105 USA
734-665-4601
jillault@umich.edu
jillault.com

# Debbie Babin

1111 Thompson Court
St. Leonard, Maryland  20685  USA
410-586-3305
debbiebabin@studioquilts.com
www.studioquilts.com

Passion Tree
© 2009
10" x 10"
25 x 25 cm

# Roberta Renee Baker

Photo: Sibila Savage

Ascension of the Butterfly Women
© 2008
38" x 34"
97 x 86 cm

3814 Everett Avenue
Oakland, California 94602 USA
510-333-1528 • Fax: 510-891-7107
robertareneebaker@yahoo.com
www.artquiltsbyrobertabaker.com

# Sharon Leigh Baker

692 N. Echo Hawk Way
Eagle, Idaho  83616  USA
208-938-1715
sbaker@kapamaker.com
www.kapamaker.com

The Ribbon Shop at the Angeles Market
© 2007
51" x 48"
130 x 122 cm

# Deborah Baldwin

DigiLily
© 2008
40" x 43"
102 x 109 cm

1020 S. Gunderson
Oak Park, Illinois 60304 USA
708-848-2541
debbdesigns@sbcglobal.net
www.debbaldwindesigns.com

# Lynn Bartley

3629 Wright Road S.W.
Rochester, Minnesota  55902  USA
507-244-0629
bartley.lynn@gmail.com
www.lynnbartley.com

Incidentally...
© 2008
22" x 19"
56 x 48 cm

# Sharon M.W. Bass

Hot Poppies
© 2009
39" x 30"
99 x 76 cm

1727 West 27th Terrace
Lawrence, Kansas 60046 USA
785-842-2285
bass@mac.com
www.smwbass.com

# Linda Beach

Photo: Danny Daniels Photography

22909 Green Garden Drive
Chugiak, Alaska 99567 USA
907-688-3335
lbeach@gci.net
www.lindabeachartquilts.com

Home Before Dark
© 2007
51" x 39"
130 x 99 cm

# Alice Beasley

Fuld's Gold
© 2008
37" x 28"
94 x 71 cm

1018 Park Lane
Oakland, California  94610  USA
510-465-6543 • Cell: 510-543-4763
abeasley@sbcglobal.net
www.alicebeasley.com

# Nancy G. Beckerman

26 White Birch Road
Pound Ridge, New York  10576  USA
914-764-8106
nancybgb@verizon.net

The Checkered Heart Feels No Pain
© 2008
15" x 15"
38 x 38 cm

# Christi Beckmann

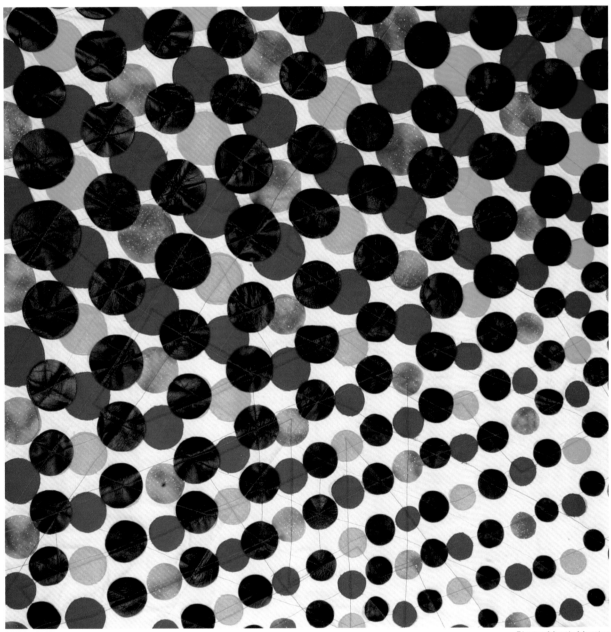

Photo: Murth Murthy

Geometrix
© 2008
38" x 36"
97 x 91 cm

5519 Foothills Drive
Berthoud, Colorado  80513  USA
970-532-7100
christibeckmann@yahoo.com
www.freereinarts.com

# Marilyn Belford

543 South Street
Chenango Forks, New York  13746  USA
607-692-4484
marilynbelford@earthlink.net
www.marilynbelford.com

Medea and Sons
© 2007
45" x 33"
114 x 84 cm

# Mary Beth Bellah

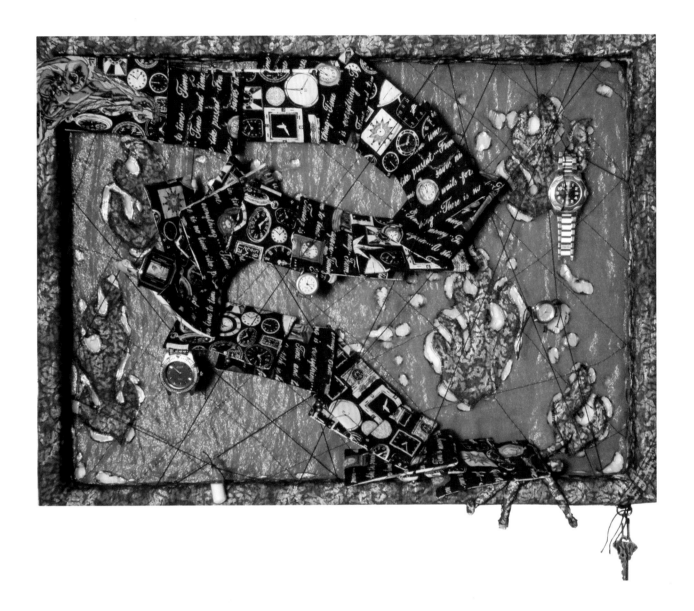

Pellmell to Hell | 1855 Arrowhead Valley Road
© 2008 | Charlottesville, Virginia  22903  USA
19" x 25" | 434-409-9213
48 x 64 cm | mb@marybethbellah.com
| www.marybethbellah.com

# Sue Benner

Photo: Eric Neilsen

8517 San Fernando Way
Dallas, Texas 75218 USA
214-324-3550
suebenner@aol.com
www.suebenner.com

Body Parts (Zebra Sleeve, Paisley Sleeve)
© 2007
81" x 61"
206 x 155 cm

# Astrid Hilger Bennett

Urban Salsa
© 2008
40" x 62"
102 x 158 cm

909 Webster Street
Iowa City, Iowa 52240 USA
319-430-3183
bennettic@mchsi.com
www.astridhilgerbennett.com

# Regina Benson

Photo: John Bonath

14154 W. 1st Drive
Golden, Colorado  80401  USA
303-278-0413
regina-b@comcast.net
www.reginabenson.com

Roan Plateau
© 2008
12" x 12" x 3"
30 x 30 x 8 cm

# Liz Berg

California Dreaming 2: Southern California
© 2008
26" x 44"
66 x 112 cm

20397 Forest Avenue
Castro Valley, California  94546  USA
lizberg@sbcglobal.net
www.lizbergartquilts.com

# Charlotte Bird

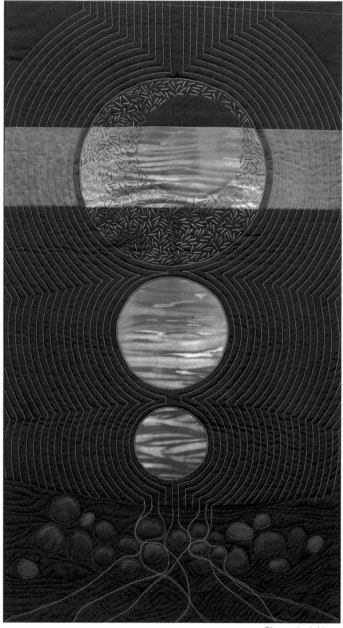

Photo: Jack Yonn

2633 Reynard Way
San Diego, California 92103 USA
619-294-7236 • Fax: 619-294-6873
Cbird2400@aol.com
www.birdworks-fiberarts.com

Zen Moon
© 2008
25" x 14"
64 x 36 cm

# Eszter Bornemisza

Photo: Aron Levendel

Depends...
© 2008
61" x 35"
155 x 88 cm

Varosmajor u. 52
1122 Budapest
Hungary
3630-3995728
eszter@bornemisza.com
www.bornemisza.com

# Tammie Bowser

917 Fremont Avenue
PMB 138
South Pasadena, California 91030 USA
626-799-5998 • Fax: 626-243-4423
tammie@mosaicquilt.com
www.tammiebowser.com

Bob
© 2008
30" x 30"
76 x 76 cm

# Laurie Brainerd

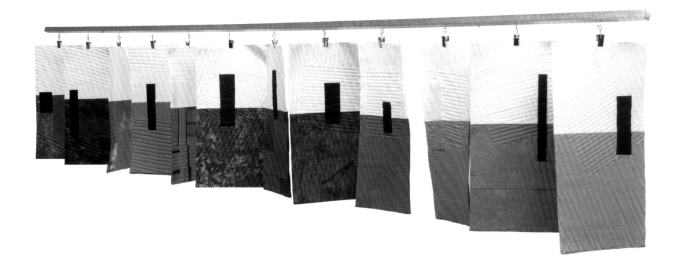

Dance | 152 E. Pecan Street, No. 1003
© 2008 | San Antonio, Texas  78205  USA
14" x 7" x 78" | 210-219-3582
36 x 17 x 198 cm | lauriebrainerd@gmail.com
| www.lauriebrainerd.typepad.com

# Ann Brauer

Photo: John Polak

2 Conway Street
Shelburne Falls, Massachusetts  01370  USA
413-625-8605
ann@annbrauer.com
www.annbrauer.com

hills, fields, river and two trees: scenes from
western Massachusetts
© 2008
48" x 110"
122 x 279 cm

# Melani Kane Brewer

Photo: Gerhard Heidersberger

Nestor ~ A Little Green Heron
© 2009
23" x 36"
58 x 91 cm

3801 Bridge Road
Cooper City, Florida  33026  USA
954-431-8700
melanibrewerstudio@att.net
www.melanibrewer.com

# Eliza Brewster

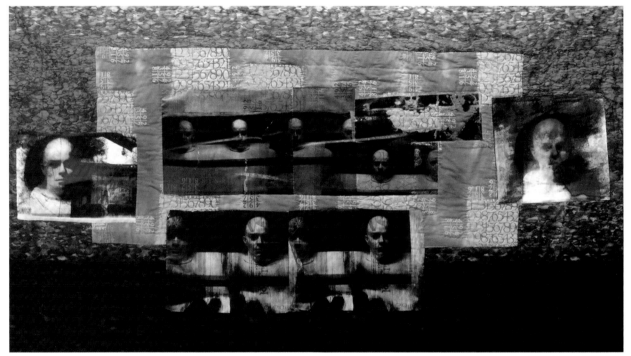

Photo: Sam Brewster

1991 Great Bend Turnpike
Honesdale, Pennsylvania  18431  USA
570-448-2904  •  Fax: 570-448-3904
elizal@msn.com
www.fineartquilts.com

Double Jeopardy
© 2008
28" x 48"
71 x 122 cm

# Kathie Briggs

Visitor
© 2008
39" x 28"
99 x 71 cm

13595 Phelps Road
Charlevoix, Michigan  49720  USA
231-547-4971
kathie@kathiebriggs@com
www.kathiebriggs.com

# Jack Brockette

Jackethouse Originals
7358 Fieldgate Drive
Dallas, Texas 75230 USA
214-365-0692
jack@brockette.com
www.brockette.com

Through A Glass Darkly
© 2008
39" x 39"
99 x 99 cm

# Shelley Brucar

Silver Birch
© 2008
36" x 41"
91 x 104 cm

1399 Larchmont Drive
Buffalo Grove, Illinois  60089  USA
847-921-4364
shelley@handmade-memories.com
www.handmade-memories.com

# Melinda Bula

3221 Woedee Drive
El Dorado Hills, California  95762  USA
916-939-0375 • Cell: 916-768-3215
melbula@comcast.net
www.melindabula.com

Splendor In the Grass
© 2007
41" x 59"
104 x 150 cm

# Marianne Burr

Photo: Frank Ross

Chocolate Truffles
© 2008
48" x 36"
122 x 91 cm

566 Olympic View Drive
Coupeville, Washington  98239  USA
360-678-6119
www.marianneburr.com

# Betty Busby

Photo: Alan Mitchell Photography

14306 Oakwood Place
Albuquerque, New Mexico  87123  USA
505-275-9511
fbusby3@comcast.net
http://home.comcast.net/~bbusbyarts/site

Cytology
© 2008
58" x 47"
147 x 119 cm

# Leslie Commons Carabas

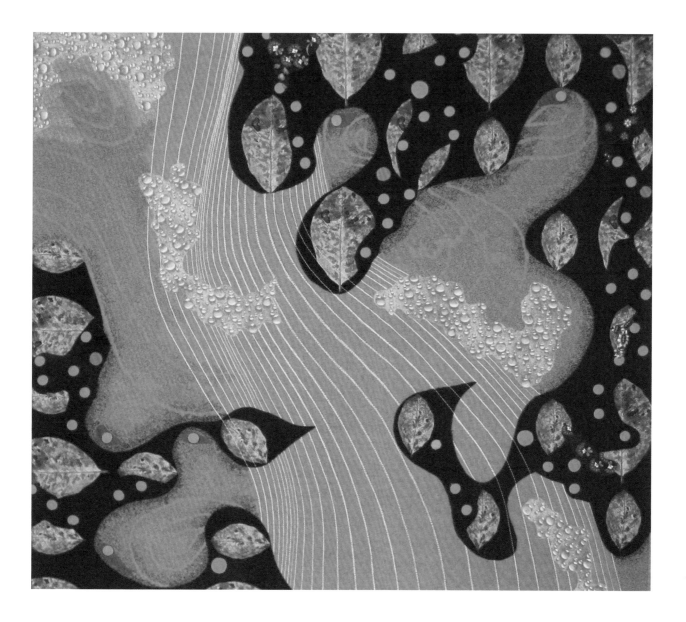

Fantasy 3
© 2008
36" x 39"
91 x 99 cm

22686 Meadow Lane
Sonora, California 95370 USA
209-532-0653
lesliec@carabas.org
www.leslie.carabas.org

# Ruth Carden

1227 Manucy Road
Fernandina Beach, Florida 32034 USA
904-277-1562
Ragcarden@aol.com

Threnody
© 2007
33" x 29"
84 x 74 cm

# Marilyn Chaffee

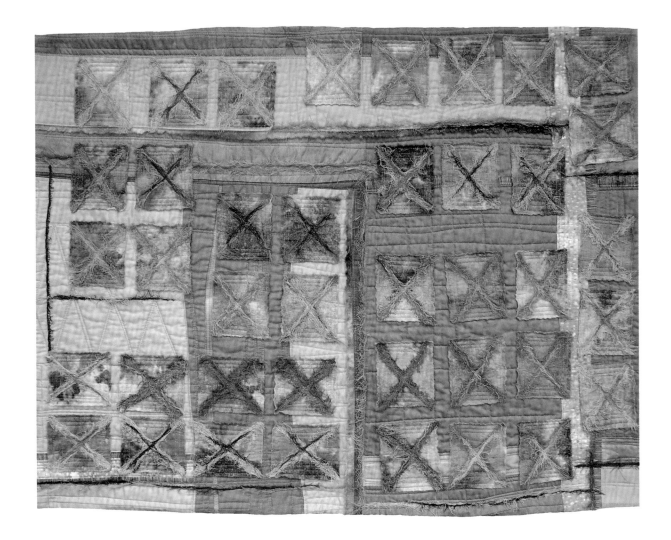

Marking Time #4: Contemplating
a Forty Year Milestone
© 2008
24" x 31"
61 x 79 cm

12896 Stone Canyon Road
Poway, California 92064 USA
858-487-4398
Marilyn@chaffeestudio.com
www.marilyn.chaffeestudio.com

# Hollis Chatelain

Photo: Lynn Ruck Photography

909 Lawrence Road
Hillsborough, North Carolina  27278  USA
919-732-5119 • Fax: 919-732-5730
hollis@hollisart.com
www.hollisart.com

Hope For Our World
© 2007
81" x 81"
206 x 206 cm

# Lisa M. Chipetine

Photo: Karen Bell

Waves of Emotion: Relief
© 2008
42" x 54"
107 x 137 cm

707 Maple Place
West Hempstead, New York  11552  USA
516-857-3228  •  Fax: 212-202-3647
lisa@threadplay.com
www.threadplay.com

# Paula Chung

P.O. Box 338
Zephyr Cove, Nevada  89448  USA
775-588-3865
paula@paulachung.com
www.paulachung.com

Dark Rose 5
© 2008
54" x 70"
137 x 178 cm

# Rosemary Claus-Gray

Blue
© 2008
31" x 20"
79 x 51 cm

Rt. 1 Box 1605
Doniphan, Missouri  63935  USA
573-354-2624
rosemary@semo.net
www.rosemaryclaus-gray.com

# Jette Clover

Photo: Fotostudio Leemans

Generaal van Merlenstraat 9
2600 Antwerpen
Belgium
0032-3-2397437
jette@jetteclover.com
www.jetteclover.com

Letter Landscape 14
© 2008
56" x 52"
142 x 132 cm

# Linda Colsh

Photo: Fotostudio Leemans

Drawing on the Mist
© 2008
40" x 40"
102 x 102 cm

PSC 81 Box 51    or
APO AE 09724
USA

+322-757-2580
linda.colsh@gmail.com
www.lindacolsh.com

Sijsjeslaan 32
B-3078 Everberg
Belgium

# Joanell Connolly

6171 Sydney Drive
Huntington Beach, California 92647 USA
714-893-4352
joanell@joanell.com
www.joanell.com

Sees
© 2007
36" x 21"
91 x 53 cm

# Jennifer Conrad

Photo: Jeff Conrad, Imagine Photography

Perennial Paradise
© 2009
36" x 28"
91 x 71 cm

N4429 1055th Street
Prescott, Wisconsin  54021  USA
715-792-2772 • Fax: 877-884-5875
jconrad@designsbyjconrad.com
www.designsbyjconrad.com

# Judith Content

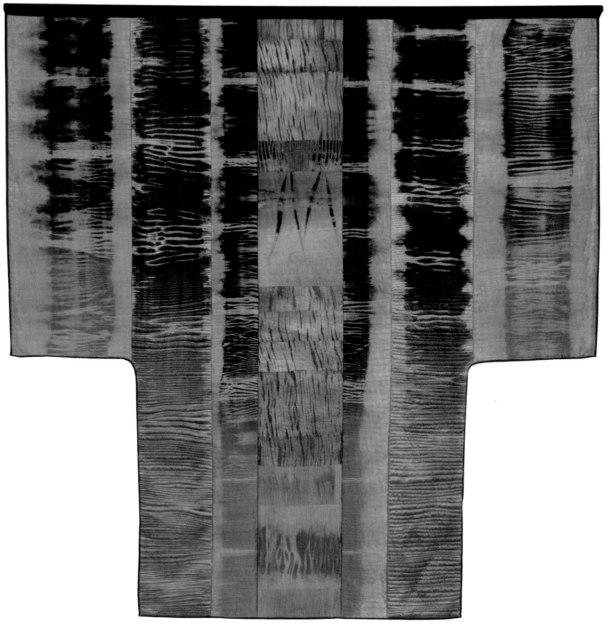

Photo: James Dewrance

827 Matadero Avenue
Palo Alto, California  94306  USA
650-857-0289
judithcontent@earthlink.net

Apparition
© 2008
73" x 70"
185 x 178 cm

# Nancy G. Cook

Ankle Twister | 6501 Brookfield Place
© 2009 | Charlotte, North Carolina  28270  USA
8" x 8" | 704-366-9643
20 x 20 cm | ngcook1@bellsouth.net
| www.nancygcook.com

# Cindy Cooksey

13 Bull Run
Irvine, California  92620  USA
714-838-2821
cwcooksey@sbcglobal.net
www.cindycooksey.com

A Dance to Spring
© 2008
40" x 40"
102 x 102 cm

# Quinn Zander Corum

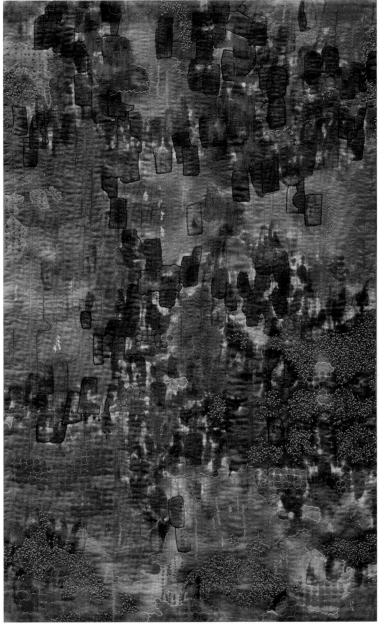

Photo: Bill Bachhuber

Census Report
© 2008
42" x 26"
107 x 66 cm

2825 N.E. 15th Avenue
Portland, Oregon 97212 USA
503-284-6507
corum@mindspring.com
www.quinnzandercorum.com

# Jean McLaughlin Cowie

29 Buffalo Bur Road
Silver City, New Mexcio  88022  USA
575-937-5843
jean@paintedrockquiltdesign.com
www.paintedrockquiltdesign.com

Cholla in Bloom
© 2008
43" x 38"
109 x 97 cm

# Robin Cowley

Photo: Don Tuttle Photography

Winter Landscape | 2451 Potomac Street
© 2008 | Oakland, California  94602  USA
20" x 20" | 510-530-1134 • Fax: 510-482-9465
51 x 51 cm | art@robincowley.com
| www.robincowley.com

# Dena Crain

P.O. Box 1141
Nakuru  20100
Kenya
+254-733-782147
dena@denacrain.com
www.denacrain.com

Bubbles III
© 2007
31" x 38"
79 x 97 cm

# Lenore Crawford

The DaVincis Rode
© 2008
24" x 20"
61 x 51 cm

2023 Ashman Street
Midland, Michigan  48640  USA
989-708-9390
lenore@lenorecrawford.com
www.lenorecrawford.com

# Denise A. Currier

8733 E. Russell Street
Mesa, Arizona  85207  USA
480-964-6019
DeniseACurrier@msn.com
www.DeniseACurrier.com

In the Ballscape
© 2007
28" x 23"
71 x 58 cm

# Margaret Cusack

Photo: Frank Cusack

Obama
© 2009
12" x 12"
30 x 30 cm

124 Hoyt Street in Boerum Hill
Brooklyn, New York 11217 USA
718-237-0145
cusackart@aol.com
www.margaretcusack.com

# Judy B. Dales

Photo: Karen Bell

2254 Craftsbury Road
P.O. Box 166
Greensboro, Vermont  05841  USA
802-533-7733 • Fax: 802-533-7783
judy@judydales.com
www.judydales.com

Floral Form III
© 2008
48" x 35"
122 x 89 cm

# Dee Danley-Brown

Crow 2 | 6694 Indian Drive
© 2009 | Magalia, California  95954  USA
14" x 11" | 530-877-1143  •  Cell: 530-680-8708
36 x 28 cm | deedanbr@joshuanet.com
| www.fabricfriendsstudio.com

# Yael David-Cohen

Photo: Max Alexander

175 West Heath Road | Butterflies
London NW3 7TT | © 2007
United Kingdom | 55" x 43"
+44 2084587988 | 140 x 110 cm
mail@simonyael.co.uk |
www.yaeldc.co.uk |

# Fenella Davies

Venetian Reflections
© 2008
40" x 43"
102 x 109 cm

3 Brock Street
Bath, N. Somerset  BA1 2LN
United Kingdom
0044 (0)1225 310369
Cell:  07887 642290
fenelladavies@btinternet.com
www.fenelladavies.com

# Jacque Davis

Photo: Gerard Reuter

8157 Jefferson Road
Freeburg, Illinois 62243 USA
618-363-9653
jacque@jacquedavis.com
www.jacquedavis.com

The Opening
© 2009
16" x 38 "
41 x 97 cm

# Sue Dennis

Photo: Bob Dennis

Anthills - Silent Cities
© 2008
27" x 48"
69 x 122 cm

31 Shelley Street
Sunnybank 4109, Queensland
Australia
+61 7 33454994
info@suedennis.com
www.suedennis.com

# Ellen Deschatres

2453 Indian Tree Run
Wildwood, Missouri 63038 USA
636-405-1704
eldescha@gmail.com
www.ellendeschatres.com

Couldn't Be Happier
© 2008
24" x 10" x 20"
61 x 25 x 50 cm

# Dianne Vottero Dockery

Moonlit Canyon
© 2009
12" x 12"
30 x 30 cm

83 Boy Scout Road
Kutztown, Pennsylvania  19530  USA
610-683-6137
dvdathome@yahoo.com
www.diannevotterodockery.com

# Pat Dolan

1108 Mayberry Lane
State College, Pennsylvania  16801  USA
814-308-8287
pat.dolan.artist@gmail.com
www.pat-dolan.com

Red Ribbons
© 2007
43" x 32"
109 x 81 cm

# Chiaki Dosho

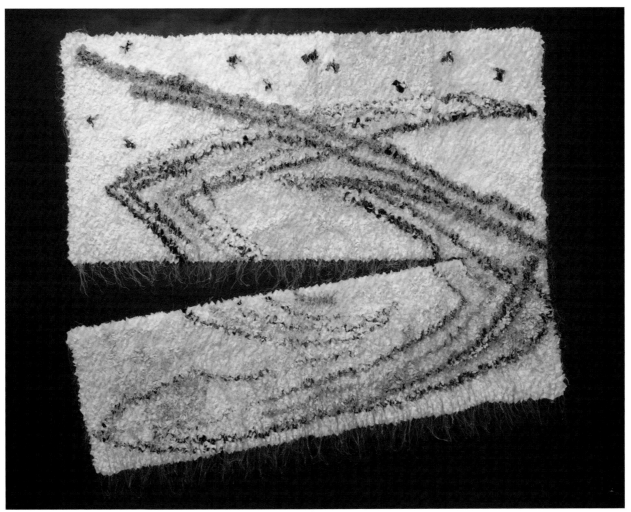

Photo: Toshihiro Kobe

Over The Galaxy | 4-1-1-221, Hakusan
© 2007 | Asao-ku, Kawasaki-shi
67" x 87" | Kanagawa-ken  215-0014
170 x 220 cm | Japan
| +81-44-987-9120
| chiakidoshoart@mac.com
| http://web.mac.com/chiakidoshoart/

# Eileen Doughty

9701 Rhapsody Drive
Vienna, Virginia  22181  USA
703-938-6916
artist@DoughtyDesigns.com
www.DoughtyDesigns.com

Moon Dance
© 2008
51" x 42"
130 x 107 cm

# Brian Dykhuizen

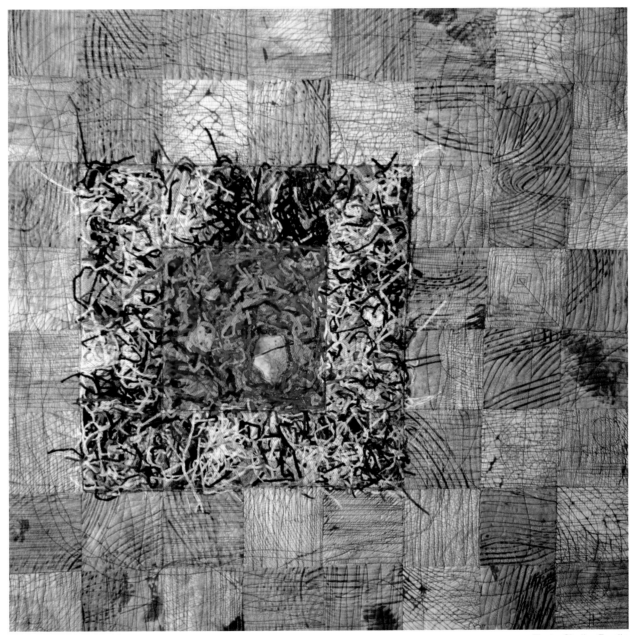

Photo: Shelley Emslie

Rabbit Retina 3
© 2008
48" x 48"
122 x 122 cm

25 Trillium Way
Kalispell, Montana 59901 USA
406-257-0175
bswcs5@yahoo.com
www.briandykhuizen.com

# Susan Else

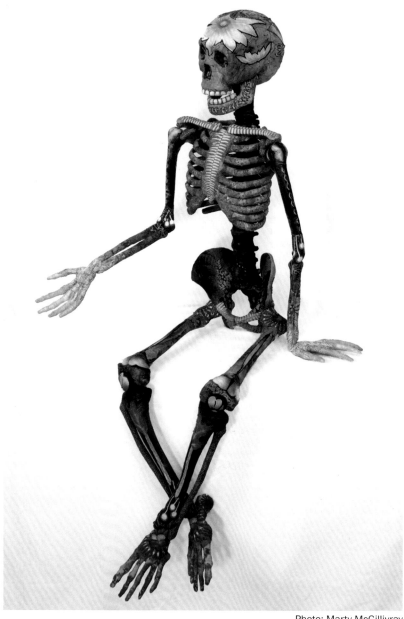

Photo: Marty McGillivray

126 Escalona Drive
Santa Cruz, California 95060 USA
831-423-0515
selse@pacbell.net
www.susanelse.com

Nothing To Fear
© 2008
49" x 30" x 27"
124 x 76 x 69 cm

# Noriko Endo

Photo: Masaru Nomura

Radiant Reflections
© 2008
66" x 80"
168 x 203 cm

4-18-33 Fujisaki, Narashino
Chiba  275-0017
Japan
81-47-477-7462
norikoendojp@yahoo.co.jp

# Susan Ennis

Photo: Rick Wells

720 Second Street
Humble, Texas 77338 USA
281-793-8695
ennissusan@embarqmail.com

Memories of A Dream
© 2008
12" x 12"
30 x 30 cm

# Nancy N. Erickson

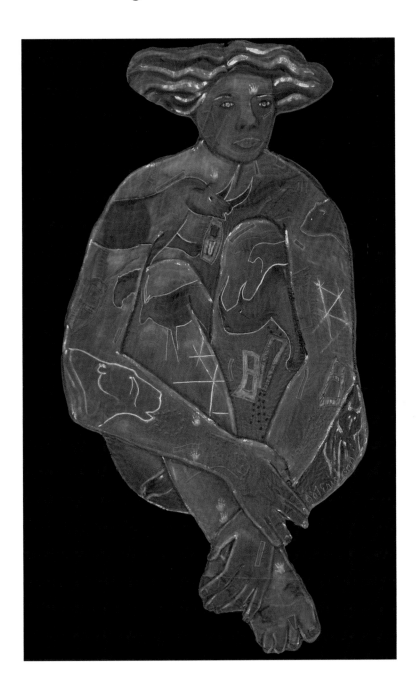

Sibyl of Lascaux
© 2007
66" x 33"
168 x 84 cm

3250 Pattee Canyon Road
Missoula, Montana 59803 USA
406-549-4671
nancron@aol.com
www.nancyericksoncom

# Wendy Feldberg

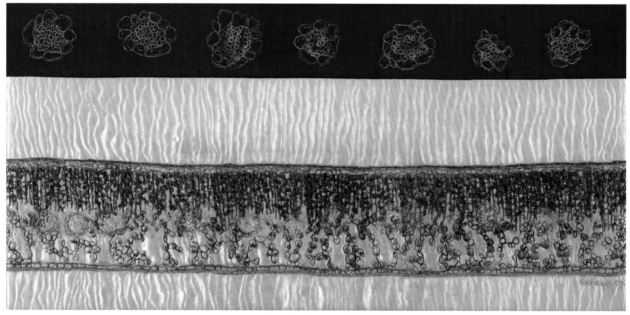

Photo: Andrew Balfour

20 Wilton Crescent
Ottawa, Ontario  K1S 2T5
Canada
613-232-1829
wendy.feldberg@sympatico.ca
www.wendyfeldberg.ca

Celluminations 5
© 2008
12" x 24"
30 x 61 cm

# Deborah Fell

Reclamation Green
© 2009
24" x 55"
61 x 140 cm

1412 Raintree Woods
Urbana, Illinois  61802  USA
217-384-0544
art@deborahfell.com
www.deborahfell.com

# Cheryl Dineen Ferrin

22258 Bluebird Avenue
Mattawan, Michigan 49071  USA
269-668-4604 • Cell: 269-267-7993
cheryl@cdineenferrin.com
www.cdineenferrin.com

Motorcyclist Portrait Project: Kevin
© 2009
96" x 46"
243 x 117 cm

# Clairan Ferrono

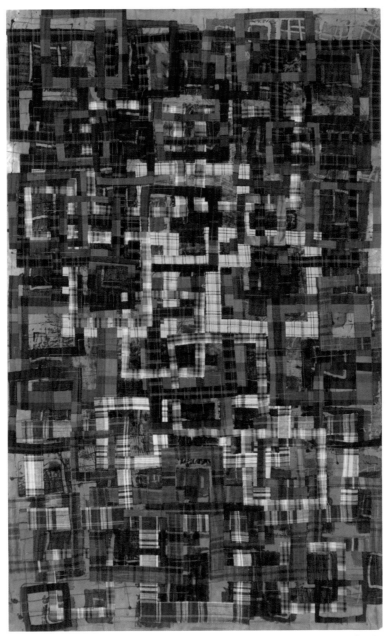

Photo: Tom Van Eynde

Grape Harvest: Tuscany
© 2007
36" x 22"
91 x 56 cm

5432 Dorchester Ave
Chicago, Illinois 60615 USA
773-667-4403 • Fax: 773-493-1552
fabric8tions@hotmail.com
www.fabric8tions.net

# Linda Filby-Fisher

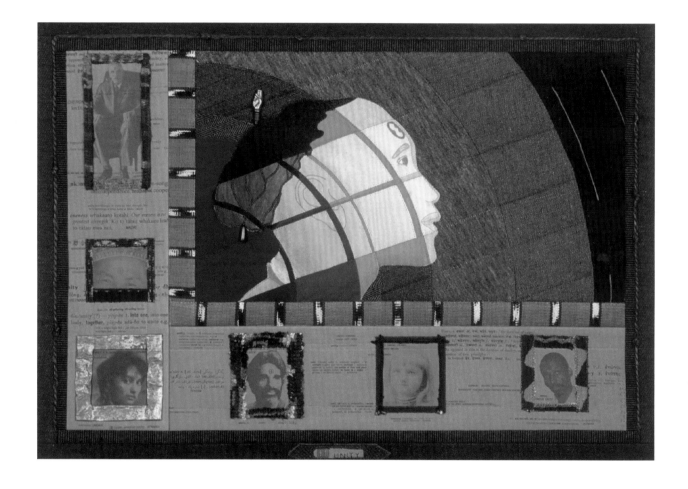

6401 W. 67th Street
Overland Park, Kansas 66202 USA
913-722-2608 • Fax: 913-722-0391
lffkc@yahoo.com
kansasartquilters.org

Unity 2 Medicine Wheel series
© 2007
18" x 25"
46 x 64 cm

# Jamie Fingal

Apron as Personal Armor
© 2008
38" x 27"
97 x 69 cm

1500 E. Katella Avenue, Suite K
Orange, California  92867  USA
714-744-4982
Jamie.Fingal@gmail.com
www.JamieFingal.com

# Tommy Fitzsimmons

642 Forestwood Drive
Romeoville, Illinois  60446  USA
Cell: 630-319-7553
tommygirl@americanstair.net
www.tommysartquilts.com

Eclipse
© 2008
39" x 39"
99 x 99 cm

# Floris Flam

Photo: Paul Seder

Altered Perspectives
© 2008
36" x 30"
91 x 76 cm

5450 Whitley Park Terrace, Apt. 104
Bethesda, Maryland 20814 USA
301-530-7773
floris@florisflam.com
www.florisflam.com

# Betty Cabell Ford

12704 Rigdale Terrace
Silver Spring, Maryland 20904 USA
301-384-4683 • Cell: 301-526-4815
bcford@comcast.net
www.bettyfordquilts.com

Olive Orchard
© 2008
16" x 27"
41 x 69 cm

# Barb Forrister

Life's A Beach
© 2009
26" x 30"
66 x 76 cm

4012 Tecate Trail
Austin, Texas  78739  USA
512-672-9014
bjforrister@sbcglobal.net
www.freespiritartstudio.blogspot.com

# Karin Franzen

388 Reynolds Lane
Fairbanks, Alaska  99712  USA
907-448-2430  •  Fax: 907-488-7676
kfranzen@att.net
www.karinfranzen.com

A Time to Dance - June 4th
© 2008
49" x 44"
124 x 112 cm

# Linda Frost

Oracle Script | 1313 Raintree Place
© 2009 | Lawrence, Kansas  66044  USA
18" x 18" | 785-841-3244
46 x 46 cm | LLFrost@Sunflower.com
| www.13thStreetStudio.com

# Deb Gabel

13618 Meadow Glenn
Clarksville, Maryland  21029  USA
410-531-9047 • Fax: 410-531-9059
debra@zebrapatterns.com
www.zebrapatterns.com

Aqua Aurora
© 2008
62" x 48"
158 x 122 cm

# Linda Gass

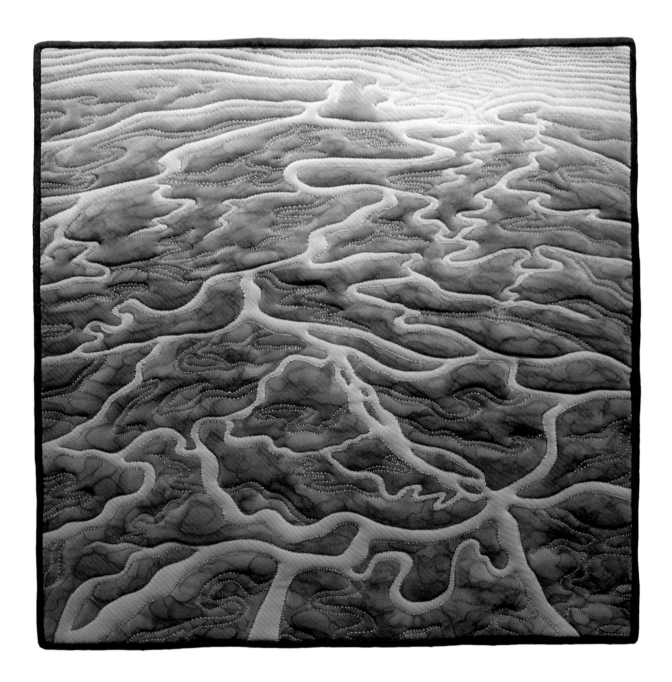

On The Edge | P.O. Box 1406
© 2008 | Los Altos, California  94023  USA
12" x 12" | 650-948-1752
30 x 30 cm | linda@lindagass.com
| www.lindagass.com

# Myrna Giesbrecht

Photo: Yuri Akuney

1849 Whistler Court
Kamloops, British Columbia  V2E 1Y6
Canada
250-828-6734
myrna@myrnagiesbrecht.com
www.myrnagiesbrecht.com

RM1
© 2007
31" x 48"
79 x 122 cm

# Martha Gilbert

Be Happy | 4663 Willowgrove Drive
© 2009 | Ellicott City, Maryland  21042  USA
37" x 27" | 410-715-3854
94 x 69 cm | info@marthagilbert.com
| www.marthagilbert.com

# Marilyn Gillis

Photo: James Barbour

6623 Spear Street
Shelburne, Vermont 05482 USA
802-985-1415
marilyngillis@gmail.com
www.marilyngillis.com

Inner Voice 4
© 2008
36" x 24"
91 x 61 cm

# Rayna Gillman

Whose Woods
© 2008
17" x 39"
43 x 99 cm

78 Sullivan Drive
West Orange, New Jersey  07052  USA
973-243-9443  •  Fax: 973-243-7296
rgillman@studio78.net
www.studio78.net

# Karen Goetzinger

5 Belgrave Road
Ottawa, Ontario  K1S 0L9
Canada
613-231-4894
quiltopia@sympatico.ca
www.karengoetzinger.com

Alpha City 10
© 2008
48" x 24"
122 x 61 cm

# Doria Anne Goocher

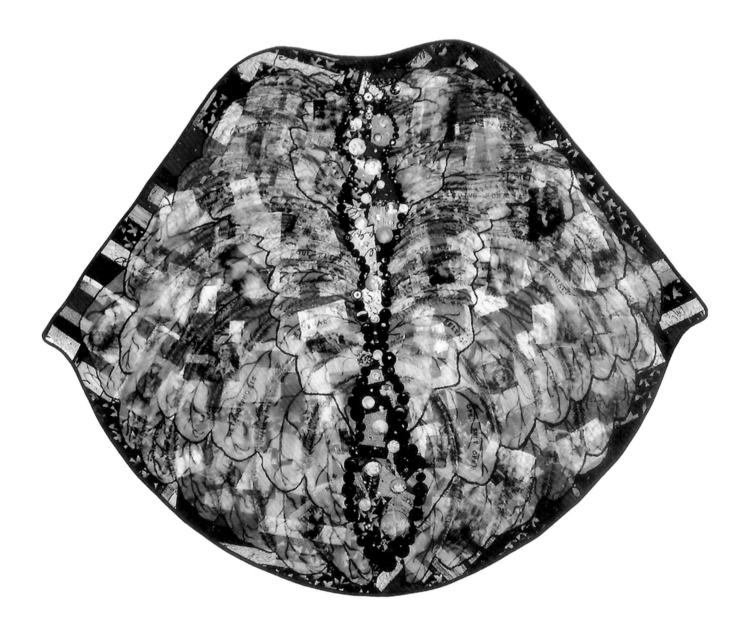

Transition
© 2007
47" x 59"
119 x 150 cm

5623 Madra Avenue
San Diego, California  92120  USA
619-582-8865
designsbydoria@aol.com
www.designsbydoria.com

# Margery Goodall

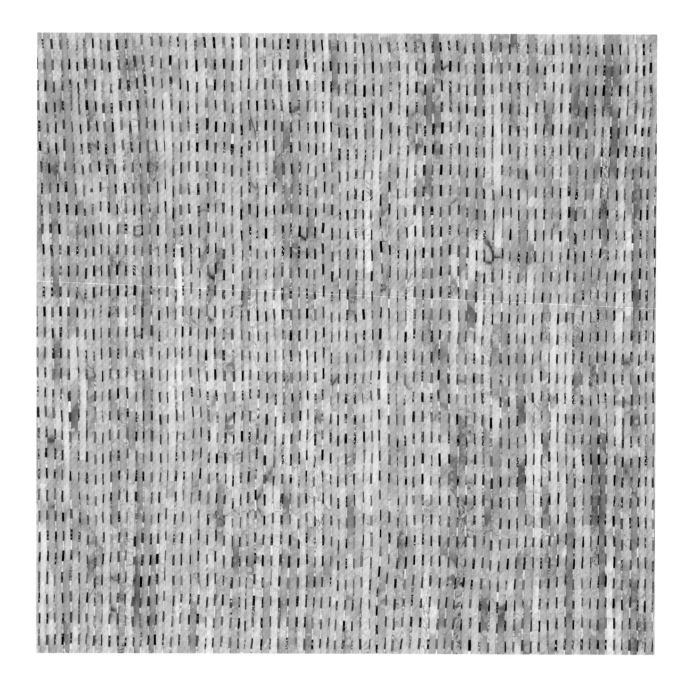

114 First Avenue
Mount Lawley, Western Australia  6050
Australia
+61 8 9271 1417  •  Fax:  +61 8 9371 6047
margery@margerygoodall.com
www.margerygoodall.com

Fire Ash
© 2007
31" x 31"
80 x 80 cm

# Valerie Goodwin

Photo: Richard Brunck

African Burial Ground II
© 2009
44" x 32"
112 x 81 cm

1700 Kathryn Drive
Tallahassee, Florida  32308  USA
850-878-9923
valeriegoodwin@comcast.net
www.quiltsbyvalerie.com

# Patricia Gould

12620 Towner Avenue N.E.
Albuquerque, New Mexico 87112 USA
505-670-6364 • Fax: 866-224-6959
patriciagould@msn.com
www.angelfiredesigns.com

Four Strong Winds
© 2008
48" x 60"
122 x 152 cm

# Sandra Gregg

Swirl 6 | 16 Watson Street
© 2008 | Cambridge, Massachusetts  02139  USA
36" x 35" | 617-864-1890
91 x 89 cm | sgregg55@doolan.net

# Deborah Gregory

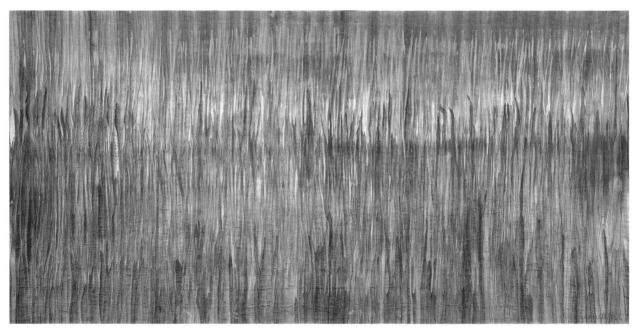

Photo: "Art and Soul"

12509 S.E. 19th Street
Bellevue, Washington  98005  USA
debkgreg@aol.com
www.deborah-gregory.com

April Colors
© 2009
21" x 42"
53 x 107 cm

# Cindy Grisdela

Photo: Gregory Staley

Playing With Colors
© 2008
45" x 54"
114 x 137 cm

708 Seneca Road
Great Falls, Virginia  22066  USA
703-421-7385 • Fax: 703-404-0382
cpgrisdela@gmail.com
www.cindygrisdela.com

# Cara Gulati

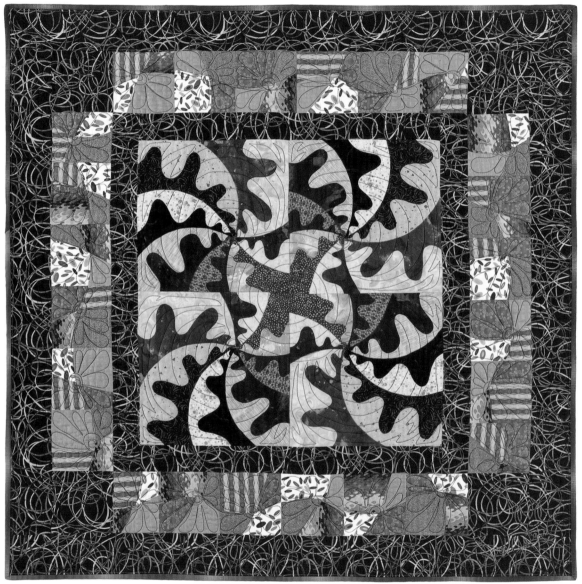

Photo: Gregory Case

P.O. Box 6640
San Rafael, California  94903  USA
415-662-2121
Cara@DoodlePress.com
www.DoodlePress.com

Rainbow Undulations
© 2009
40" x 40"
102 x 102 cm

# Gloria Hansen

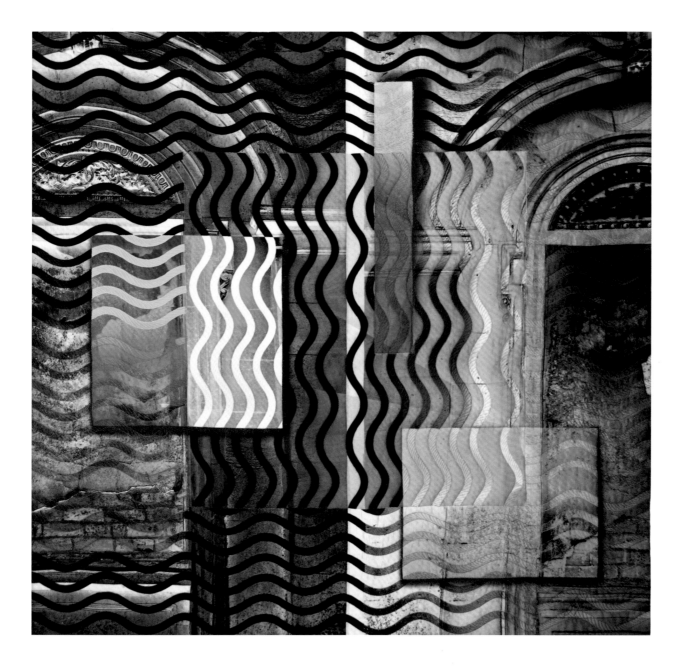

Witley Decay | 89 Oak Creek Road
© 2008 | East Windsor, New Jersey  08520  USA
40" x 39" | 609-448-7818
102 x 99 cm | gloria@gloderworks.com
| www.gloriahansen.com

# MarDee Hansen

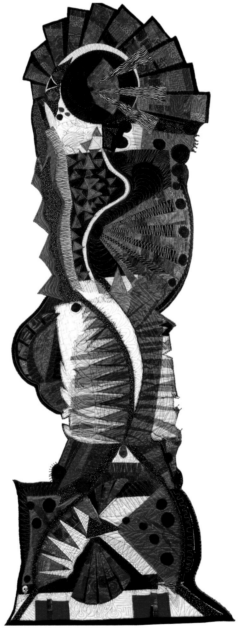

Photo: Paula Goodbar

16 N. Adams Street
Eugene, Oregon  97402  USA
541-870-5427
mardee@mardeemania.com
www.MarDeeMania.com

Screaming Red
© 2008
72" x 27"
183 x 69 cm

# Tove Pirajá Hansen

New Beginnings: hope, light, life and will   |   Mattrupvej 4
© 2008   |   DK 8765 Klovborg,
35" x 44"   |   Denmark
87 x 111 cm   |   +45 9890 4147
tovinha@yahoo.com
www.tovepirajahansen.com

# Michele Hardy

6523 Tapadero Place
Castle Rock, Colorado  80108  USA
303-663-2308
mhardy@michelehardy.com
www.michelehardy.com

Circles #28
© 2008
26" x 26"
66 x 66 cm

# Phillida Hargreaves

Rain Forest | 4060 Bath Road
© 2009 | Kingston, Ontario  K7M 4Y4
38" x 18" | Canada
97 x 46 cm | 613-389-8993
hargreavescp@sympatico.ca
www.phillidahargreaves.ca

# Lynne Harrill

105 Rae's Creek Drive
Greenville, South Carolina 29609 USA
864-292-8708
lgharrill@charter.net
www.southernhighlandguild.org/harrill/

Cross Hairs III: Kill Zone
© 2009
40" x 40"
102 x 102 cm

# Barbara O. Hartman

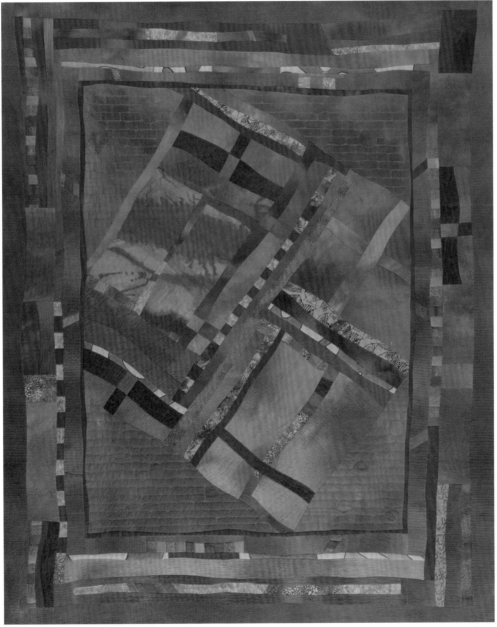

Photo: Eric Neilsen

Reclamation: Retro
© 2008
86" x 82"
218 x 208 cm

122 Red Oak Lane
Flower Mound, Texas 75028 USA
972-724-1181
barbaraohartman@aol.com
www.barbaraoliverhartman.com

# Ann Johnson Harwell

Artspace Studio #105 | Colliding Mice Galaxies NGC 4676
201 E. Davie Street | © 2008
Raleigh, North Carolina 27601 USA | 38" x 62"
919-771-8132 | 97 x 158 cm
annharwell@aol.com
www.annharwell.com

# Trisha Hassler

Photo: Nate Hassler

Just Call Me An Eternal Optimist
© 2008
22" x 21"
56 x 53 cm

416 N.W. 13th Avenue, #608
Portland, Oregon 97203 USA
503-228-8338
trisha@hasslerstudio.com
www.trishahassler.com

# Patty Hawkins

Photo: Ken Sanville Photographic Services

P.O. Box 1663
Estes Park, Colorado  80517  USA
970-577-8042
hawknestpw@gmail.com
www.pattyhawkins.com

Aspen Solace 2
© 2008
40" x 42"
198 x 102 cm

# Linda Witte Henke

Photo: Philip J. Henke

Tree of Life
© 2008
43" x 56"
109 x 142 cm

7139 Maple Bluff Lane
Indianapolis, Indiana  46236  USA
317-826-0769
linda@lindahenke.com
www.lindahenke.com

# Eva Henneberry

1769 Port Kenyon Road
Ferndale, California  95536  USA
707-786-7000
dreva@suddenlink.net
www.evahenneberry.com

Hope in the Forest
© 2008
64" x 37"
163 x 94 cm

# Anna Hergert

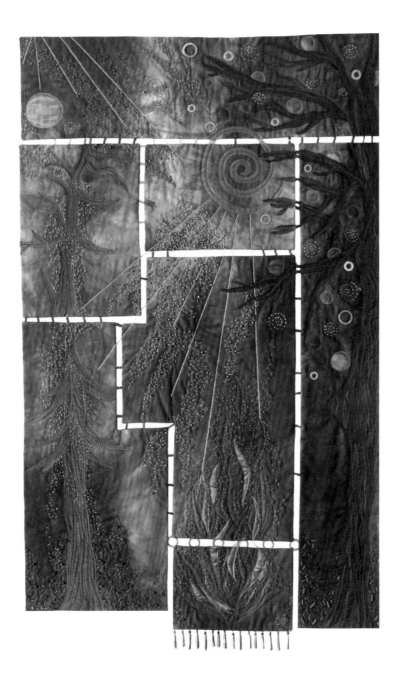

Bonavista Sunset
© 2008
37" x 22"
94 x 56 cm

P.O. Box 1274, Station Main
Moose Jaw, Saskatchewan  S6H 4P9
Canada
306-692-8058
anna@annahergert.com
www.annahergert.com

# Sandra Hoefner

Photo: Jane Aldoretta

2337 Meridian Court
Grand Junction, Colorado  81507  USA
970-812-5680
shoefner2003@yahoo.com
www.sandrahoefner.com

Goofy Foot
© 2008
71" x 50"
180 x 127 cm

# Kristin Hoelscher-Schacker

Revelation
© 2008
30" x 29"
76 x 74 cm

1365 Neal Avenue North
Lake Elmo, Minnesota 55042 USA
651-436-6862
krishoel001@mac.com

# Rosemary Hoffenberg

Photo: Joe Ofria

89 Williams Street
Wrentham, Massachusetts 02093 USA
508-384-3866 • Fax: 508-384-2075
rozeeh@comcast.net
www.rosemaryhoffenberg.com

Neighborhood
© 2008
50" x 43"
127 x 109 cm

# Sue Holdaway-Heys

Path to Serenity | 2605 Powell Avenue
© 2008 | Ann Arbor, Michigan  48104  USA
48" x 60" | 734-971-4980
122 x 152 cm | shhart@aol.com
| www.sueholdaway-heys.com

# Rose Hughes

P.O. Box 92003
Long Beach, California  90809  USA
562-985-0289
fiberart@rosehughes.com
www.rosehughes.com

Eyes Skyward
© 2009
31" x 46"
79 x 117 cm

# Cindi Huss

Wending Onward
© 2009
18" x 18"
46 x 46 cm

2117 Heatherly Road
Kingsport, Tennessee  37660  USA
423-245-5408
cindi@cindihuss.com
www.cindihuss.com

# Harumi Iida

Photo: Fumio Takahashi

Yuigahama 2-8-13
Kamakura   248-0014
Japan
+81-467-25-2593
hi_quilt@kamakuranet.ne.jp

I Pray
© 2007
40" x 40"
100 x 100 cm

# Rebecca Janes

California, USA
rjanes@mac.com
janesrebeccaart.com

Dream Catchers
© 2008
33" x 71"
167 x 180 cm

# Leslie Tucker Jenison

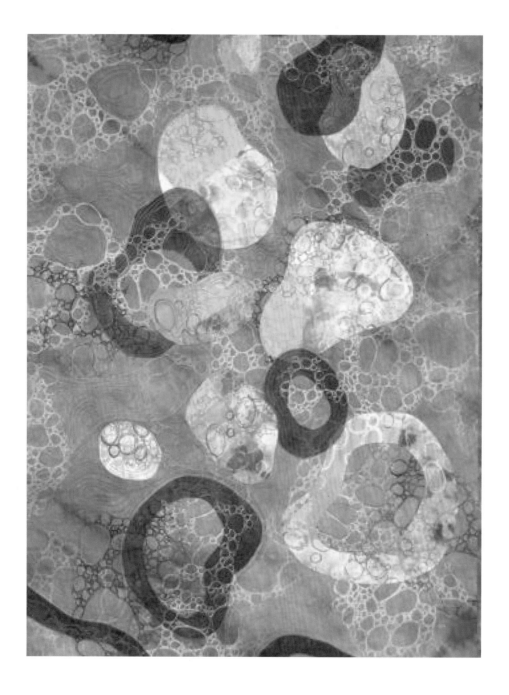

104 Ponca Bend
San Antonio, Texas  78231  USA
210-364-6067
leslie.jenison@gmail.com

InVitro#5:  Microscopy
© 2009
50" x 27"
127 x 69 cm

# Ann Johnston

Photo: Bill Bachhuber

Fragment 3 -Mountain Gyph
© 2009
14" x 13"
36 x 33 cm

P.O. Box 944
Lake Oswego, Oregon  97034  USA
503-635-6791  •  Fax: 503-675-0366
aj@annjohnston.net
www.annjohnston.net

# Gwen Jones

Photo: Peter Jones

1423 W. Highland Avenue
Chicago, Illinois  60660  USA
773-973-2784
Gwen.Jones12@gmail.com
www.peterjonesgallery.com/Gwen

The Ravine
© 2008
43" x 32"
109 x 81 cm

# Karen Kamenetzky

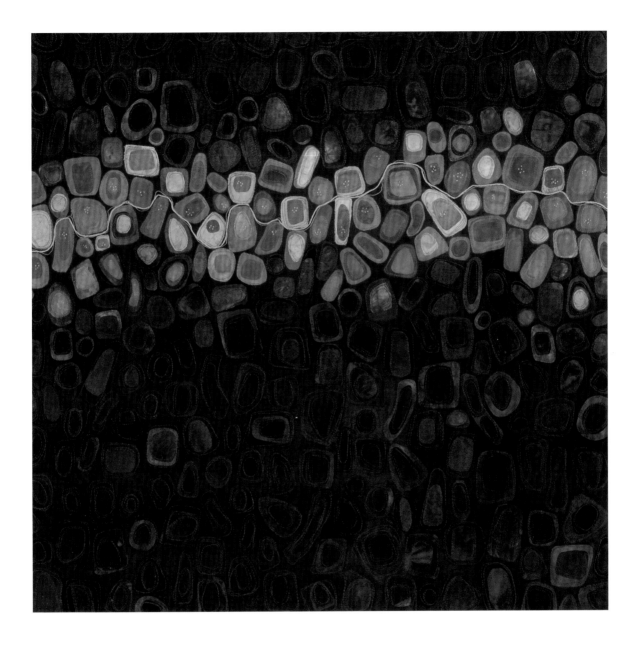

Life Goes On IV
© 2008
30" x 30"
76 x 76 cm

448 Halladay Brook Road
Brattleboro, Vermont 05301 USA
802-257-9156
kamburg@sover.net
www.karenkamenetzky.com

# Kasia

1227B Milwaukee Street
Delafield, Wisconsin  53018  USA
262-893-5510
Kasia@kasiasstudio.com
www.kasiasstudio.com

Nolan ~ LoveLight
© 2009
25" x 25"
64 x 64 cm

# Peg Keeney

Photo: Gregory Case

Reflections III
© 2008
43" x 34"
109 x 86 cm

7750 Bay Meadow Drive
Harbor Springs, Michigan  49740  USA
231-526-9597
pegkeeney@pegkeeney.com
www.pegkeeney.com

# Ann Baddeley Keister

309 Madison S.E.
Grand Rapids, Michigan 49501 USA
616-458-3849
keistera@gvsu.edu
www.annbkeister.com

Wings and Arrows
© 2008
53" x 42"
135 x 107 cm

# Misik Kim

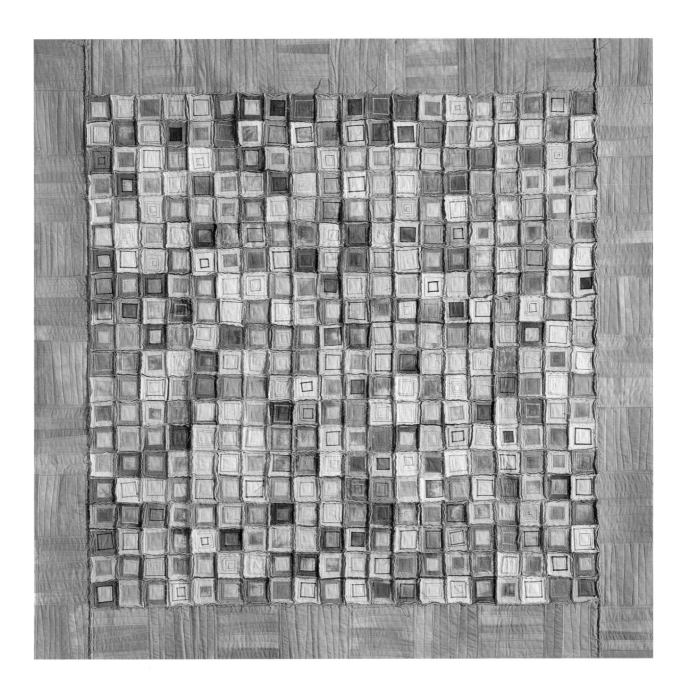

The story of my life
© 2007
52" x 53"
133 x 134 cm

# 107-2 Anguk-dong Jongro-Gu
Seoul  110-240
Korea
82-2-738-7911 • Mobile: 82-11-893-1963
kmisik@naver.com
www.naver.com/quilt4you

# Michele O'Neil Kincaid

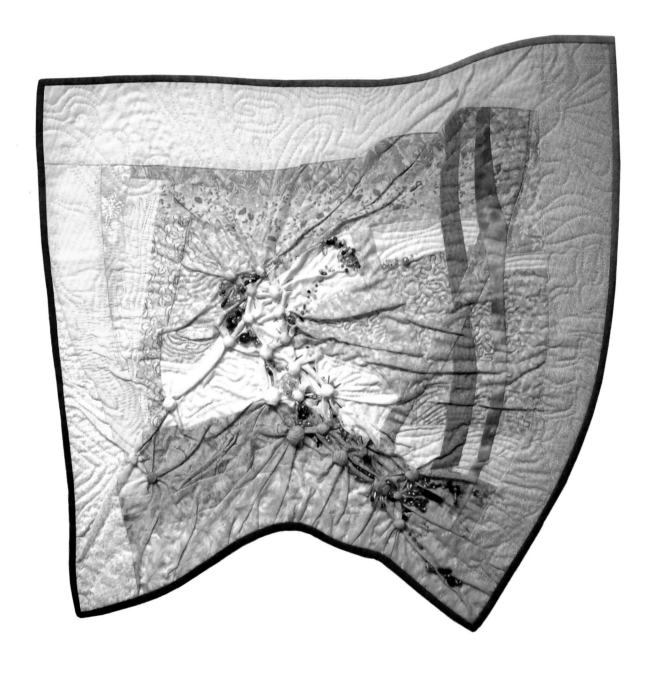

20 Hickory Way
Strafford, New Hampshire  03884  USA
603-664-2466
michele@fiberartdesigns.com
www.fiberartdesigns.com

Illusions I
© 2009
25" x 25"
64 x 64 cm

# Catherine Kleeman

Family Reunion | 915 Army Road
© 2008 | Ruxton, Maryland  21204  USA
32" x 40" | 410-321-9438
81 x 102 cm | cathy@cathyquilts.com
| www.cathyquilts.com

# Sherry Davis Kleinman

Photo: Steven Kleinman

17239 Avenida de la Herradura
Pacific Palisades, California  90272  USA
310-459-4918 • Fax: 310-459-8280
sherrykleinman@mac.com
www.sherrykleinman.com

Rehearsal
© 2008
36" x 20"
91 x 51 cm

# Chris Kleppe

Photo: Judy Smith-Kressley

A Pansy for Your Thoughts
© 2008
47" x 44"
119 x 112 cm

110 North 80th Street
Milwaukee, Wisconsin  53213  USA
414-476-3420
Kleppe.milw@juno.com

# Susan Brubaker Knapp

469 W. Center Avenue
Mooresville, North Carolina  28115  USA
704-663-0335  •  Fax: 704-662-0685
susan@bluemoonriver.com
www.bluemoonriver.com

Harbinger's Hope
© 2007
62" x 53"
158 x 135 cm

# Eleanor Kreneck

Self Portrait of the Artist as a Young Rabbit   |   3209   45th Street
© 2009   |   Lubbock, Texas   79413   USA
31" x 24"   |   806-792-7930
79 x 61 cm   |   Lyntellie@yahoo.com

# Pat Kroth

Photo: William Lemke Photography

2755 Hula Drive
Verona, Wisconsin 53593 USA
608-845-3970
krothp@juno.com
www.krothfiberart.com

Samba
© 2008
45" x 54"
114 x 137 cm

# Marcia Ann Kuehl

Kintai Kyo
© 2009
25" x 24"
64 x 61 cm

P.O. Box 7326
Capistrano Beach, California 92624 USA
949-349-9311 • Fax: 619-546-4876
ma.kuehl@gmail.com
www.polywog-fiberartstudio.com

# Pat Kumicich

46 Newbury Place
Naples, Florida  34104  USA
239-775-9517
patkumicich@me.com
www.patkumicich.com

Hmmm...
© 2008
51" x 51"
130 x 130 cm

# Denise Labadie

Photo: John Bonath

Poulnabrone Dolmen
© 2008
32" x 63"
81 x 160 cm

819 Tempted Ways Drive
Longmont, Colorado  80504  USA
720-352-0973
denise@labadiefiberart.com
www.labadiefiberart.com

# Kim Lakin

Photo: Bill Bachhuber

1925 S.E. 56th Avenue
Portland, Oregon  97215  USA
503-317-5960
klakin@comcast.net
www.kimlakin.net

Jumbo Blocks
© 2007
64" x 64"
163 x 163 cm

# Judy Langille

Photo: Peter Jacobs

Ribbon | 1 Talcott Court
© 2008 | Kendall Park, New Jersey  08824  USA
42" x 52" | 732-940-0821
107 x 132 cm | judylangille7@gmail.com

# Kim LaPolla

P.O. Box 659
Greenville, New York  12083  USA
518-966-8881 • Fax: 518-966-8754
kim@crazybydesign.com
www.crazybydesign.com

Oh Sunny Day 3
© 2007
42" x 54"
107 x 137 cm

# Carol Larson

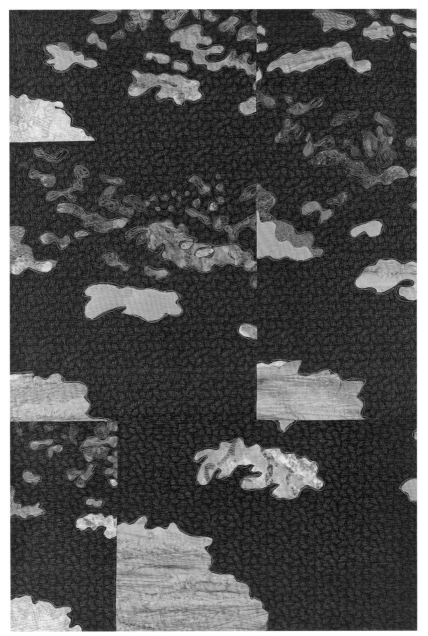

Photo: Gregory Case

Archipelago
© 2008
56" x 38"
142 x 97 cm

7 Cader Court
Petaluma, California  94952  USA
707-763-4525
cwlarson2@comcast.net
www.live2dye.com

# Janet Lasher

416 East Park Avenue
Charlotte, North Carolina  28203  USA
704-372-2437
janet@janetalasher.com
www.janetalasher.com

Bambara #6 Green Fluri
© 2008
61" x 40"
155 x 102 cm

# Mary-Ellen Latino

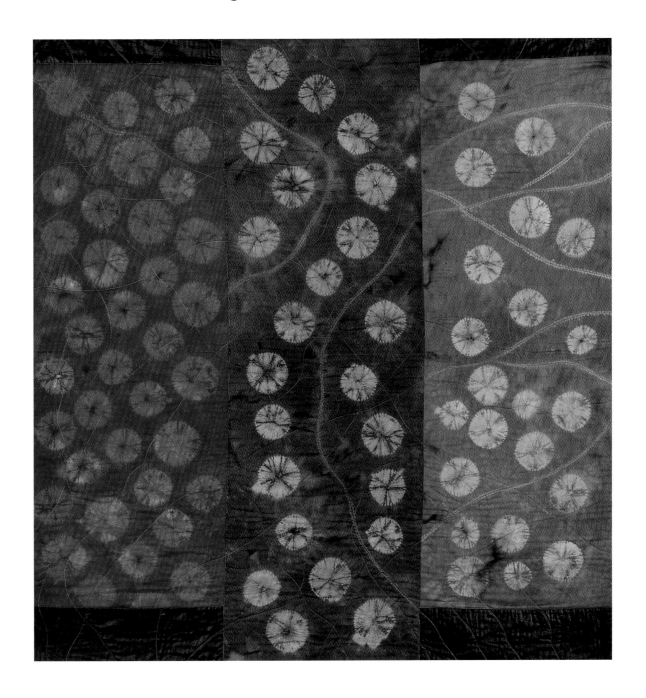

Undulations VI: Grace
© 2007
54" x 51"
137 x 130 cm

23 Sears Road
Southborough, Massachusetts  01772  USA
508-460-9584 • Cell: 508-904-0701
melsrun2000@hotmail.com
www.maryellenlatino.com

# Sandra E. Lauterbach

Photo: Stephanie Kleinman

539 Hanley Place
Los Angeles, California 90049 USA
310-476-4849
sarogier@gmail.com
www.sandralauterbach.com

Stepping Out
© 2008
43" x 36"
109 x 91 cm

# Eileen Lauterborn

Photo: Charles Parker

Writing on the Wall
© 2008
41" x 36"
104 x 91 cm

30 Frank Avenue
Farmingdale, New York 11735 USA
516-694-2819
jglandefl@aol.com
www.eileenlauterborn.com

# Catharina Breedyk Law

3045 Drummond Con 2, R R #1
Perth, Ontario  K7H 3C3
Canada
613-267-7417
catelaw@ripnet.com
www.catharinabreedyklaw.com

Mom and Me #133
© 2009
24" x 30"
61 x 76 cm

# Susan Webb Lee

Photo: Paola Nazati

Diamonds and Rust
© 2009
63" x 42"
160 x 107 cm

107 Horseshoe Trail
Barnardsville, North Carolina  28709  USA
828-606-0091
susanleestudio@aol.com
www.artquiltstudio.com

# Libby Lehman

7618 East Jordan Cove
Houston, Texas  77055  USA
713-688-7681 • Fax: 713-686-4974
threadplay@aol.com
www.libbylehman.us

Native Habitat
© 2007
49" x 49"
124 x 124 cm

# Caroll Lenthall

Epiphany Garden
© 2008
28" x 28"
71 x 71 cm

20, faubourg du Moustier
82000  Montauban
France
33 5 63 20 60 07
caroll@free.fr
www.caroll-lenthall.com

# Linda Levin

Photo: Joe Ofria

10 Brewster Road
Wayland, Massachusetts  01778  USA
508-358-4248
lindalevinart@gmail.com
www.lindalevinart.com

Central Park West Sunset
© 2008
41" x 35"
104 x 89 cm

# Ellen Lindner

Ti Plants A-Glow-Glow
© 2008
25" x 36"
64 x 91 cm

3845 Peacock Drive
Melbourne, Florida 32904 USA
321-724-8012
ellen@adventurequilter.com
www.AdventureQuilter.com

# Karen Linduska

2523 Country Club Road
Carbondale, Illinois  62901  USA
618-457-5228
linduskaartquilt@galaxycable.net
www.karenlinduska.com

Fantasy Garden
© 2007
27" x 34"
69 x 86 cm

# Denise Linet

Photo: John Anderson

Tranquility
© 2008
40" x 53"
102 x 135 cm

P. O. Box 803
22 Butterfield Road
Center Harbor, New Hampshire  03226  USA
603-253-9986
dlinet@deniselinet.com
www.DeniseLinet.com

# Phyllis Harper Loney

Photo: Tom Arter

1287 State Route 32
Round Pond, Maine  04564  USA
207-529-2310
colorphl@tidewater.net

Five Flights of Fancy
© 2008
50" x 10"
127 x 25 cm

# Karen Loprete

Four Happy Flowers | 8 Plaskon Drive Extension
© 2008 | Shelton, Connecticut 06484 USA
11" x 11" | 203-924-5623
28 x 28 cm | karen@karenloprete.com
| www.karenloprete.com

# Ann Loveless

Photo: Steve Loveless

180 Sunset Drive
Frankfort, Michigan  49635  USA
231-352-5491
annlove@charter.net
www.quiltsbyann.com

Lake Michigan
© 2009
17" x 24"
43 x 61 cm

# Wendy Lugg

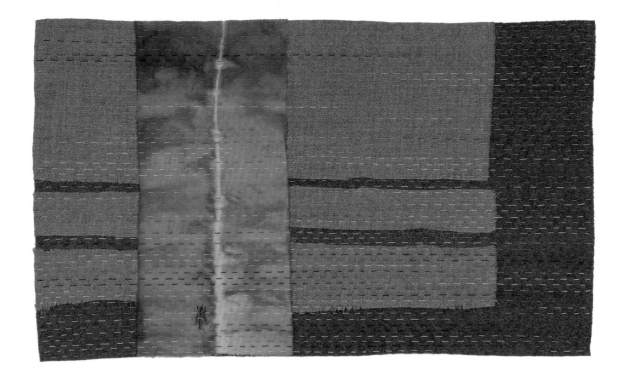

Reflections
© 2008
20" x 33"
50 x 84 cm

20 Bass Rd
Bull Creek, Western Australia  6149
Australia
+61 8 9332 7075
wendy@wendylugg.com
www.wendylugg.com

# Anne Lullie

1014 Burr Street
Lake in the Hills, Illinois  60156  USA
847-658-2294
annelullie@gmail.com
www.annelullie.com

Rose Mandala I
© 2009
45" x 45"
114 x 114 cm

# Susan Leslie Lumsden

Photo: Bruce Carr

Live Water | 221 N. Third Street
© 2008 | Thayer, Missouri  65791  USA
70" x 105" | 417-274-1561
178 x 267 cm | susan@rebelquilter.com
| www.rebelquilter.com

# Karin Lusnak

Photo: Sibila Savage

829 Stannage Avenue
Albany, California 94706 USA
510-527-7294
KLusnak@cca.edu
www.KarinLusnak.com

Latitude Red
© 2007
19" x 31"
48 x 79 cm

# Suzanne MacGuineas

Photo: David L. Smith

Dog Eat Dog World
© 2008
45" x 40"
114 x 102 cm

10521 Country Lane
Wexford, Pennsylvania  15090  USA
724-935-2976
suzanneinwexford@comcast.net

# Cherilyn Martin

Photo: Marina Rossi

Zellersacker 21-68
6546HS Nijmegen
The Netherlands
00-31-24-3785004
info@cherilynmartin.com
www.cherilynmartin.com

It's the Stones that Speak 4
© 2009
56" x 60"
142 x 152 cm

# Therese May

Photo Richard Johns

Spirit
© 2009
71" x 70"
180 x 178 cm

1556 Wawona Drive
San Jose, California  95125  USA
408-448-3247
therese@theresemay.com
www.theresemay.com

# Mary E. McBride

413 Albany Avenue
DeLand, Florida 32724 USA
386-212-5777
mrsgorgon@gmail.com
www.marymcbridearts.homestead.com

The Wrath of Mrs. Gorgon
© 2009
22" x 17"
56 x 43 cm

# Kathleen McCabe

Photo: Phil Imming

In His Shadow
© 2008
29" x 33"
74 x 84 cm

250 H Avenue
Coronado, California  92118  USA
619-435-1299 • Fax: 619-435-1298
kathmccabe@gmail.com
www.kathleenmccabecoronado.com

# Eleanor A. McCain

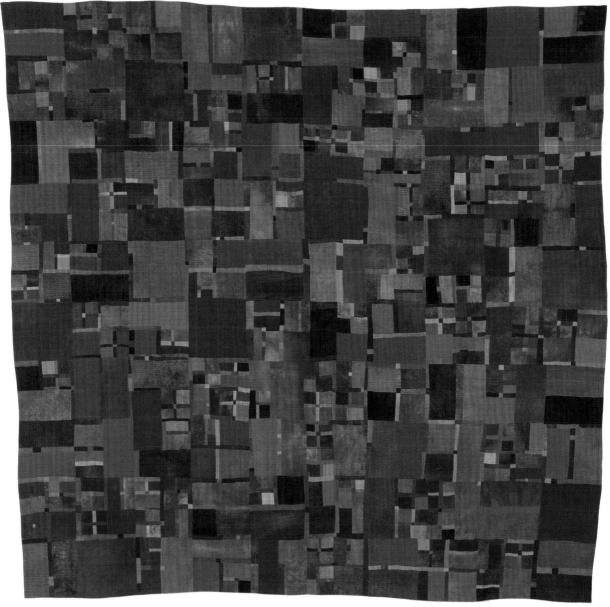

Photo: Luke Jordan

87 Meigs Drive
Shalimar, Florida 32579 USA
850-864-3815 • Fax: 850-864-3817
emccain@eleanormccain.net
www.eleanormccain.net

Green Study 2
© 2008
104" x 104"
264 x 264 cm

# Jae McDonald

Photo: Jon Christopher Meyer

Spring
© 2008
42" x 9"
107 x 23 cm

2853 Riverview Street
Eugene, Oregon  97403  USA
541-338-9212
chaicreates@comcast.net
www.jaemcdonald.com

# Judith McIrvin

946 Bryant Avenue
Colonial Beach, Virginia  22443  USA
804-410-2025
j.mcirvin@att.net
www.mcirvin.com

Volatility
© 2009
78" x 49"
198 x 124 cm

# Barbara Barrick McKie

Peacock Pride
© 2009
32" x 23"
81 x 58 cm

40 Bill Hill Road
Lyme, Connecticut  06371  USA
860-434-5222
mckieart@comcast.net
www.mckieart.com

# Salli McQuaid

Photo: Mike McQuaid

6 Rustic Bend Place
The Woodlands, Texas 77382 USA
281-292-5089
artistwriter@oplink.net
www.artistwriter.com

Coyote Night
© 2009
20" x 26"
51 x 66 cm

# Jeannette DeNicolis Meyer

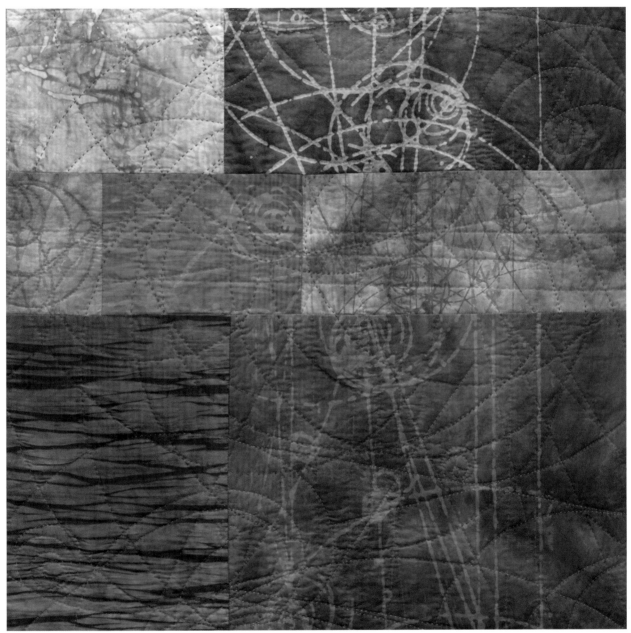

Photo: Bill Bachhuber

Essential Maps 4
© 2008
39" x 29"
99 x 74 cm

12025 S.W. Breyman Avenue
Portland, Oregon 97219 USA
503-697-8334
jdmeyer@jdmeyer.com
www.jdmeyer.com

# Libby & Jim Mijanovich

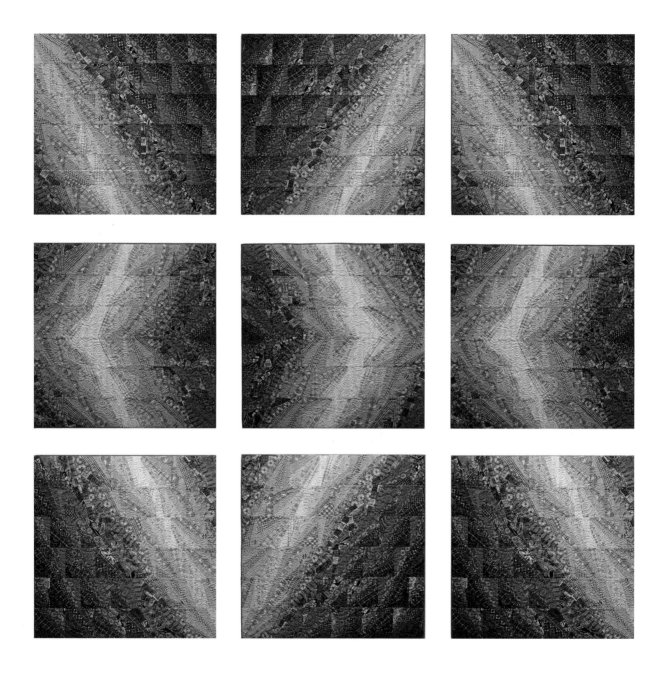

651 Long Branch Road
Marshall, North Carolina 28753 USA
828-649-0200
contact@mijafiberart.com
www.mijafiberart.com

Journey
© 2008
78" x 78"
198 x 198 cm

# Karen Miller

Photo: Don Ferguson, Shadowsmith Photographics

Winterlight
© 2008
30" x 60"
76 x 152 cm

304 N.W. 28th Street
Corvallis, Oregon  97330  USA
541-754-1573
karen@nautilus-fiberarts.com
www.nautilus-fiberarts.com

# Angela Moll

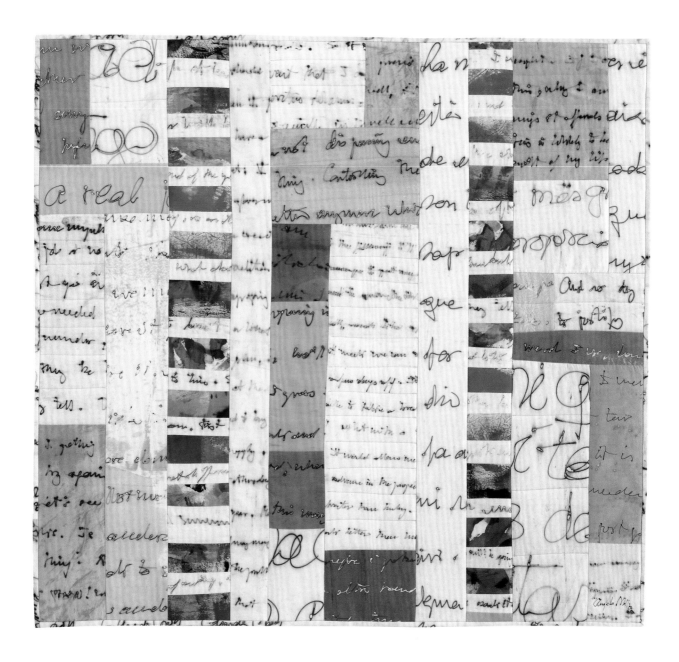

5635 W. Camino Cielo
Santa Barbara, California 92105 USA
805-683-6622
angela@angelamoll.com
www.angelamoll.com

Secret Diary: List 5
© 2008
36" x 38"
91 x 97 cm

# Nana Montgomery

Fallen Sun
© 2008
26" x 26"
66 x 66 cm

209 Hubbard Street
Santa Cruz, California 95060 USA
831-423-6804
nana@bluesharkdesign.com
www.bluesharkdesign.com

# Dottie Moore

1134 Charlotte Avenue
Rock Hill, South Carolina  29732  USA
803-327-5088
dottie@dottiemoore.com
www.dottiemoore.com

Invisible Forces
© 2008
36" x 74"
91 x 188 cm

# Lynne Morin

Moving Forward
© 2009
27" x 27"
69 x 69 cm

1 Hemlo Cres
Kanata, Ontario  K2T 1C7
Canada
613-271-0946
lynnemorin@rogers.com

# Patti Morris

61 Allan Close
Red Deer, Alberta  T4R 1A4
Canada
403-347-3247
p.tmorris@shaw.ca
www.morrisfabricartdesigns.com

Trees of The Night
© 2008
63" x 41"
160 x 104 cm

# Alison Muir

Photo: Andy Payne

Blue Gold
© 2008
39" x 35"
99 x 89 cm

Apt 3, 40 Ben Boyd Road
Neutral Bay, New South Wales  2089
Australia
+61 2 9922 2481 • Cell: +61 411 282 010
alison@muirandmuir.com.au
www.ozquiltnetwork.org.au

# Carol L. Myers

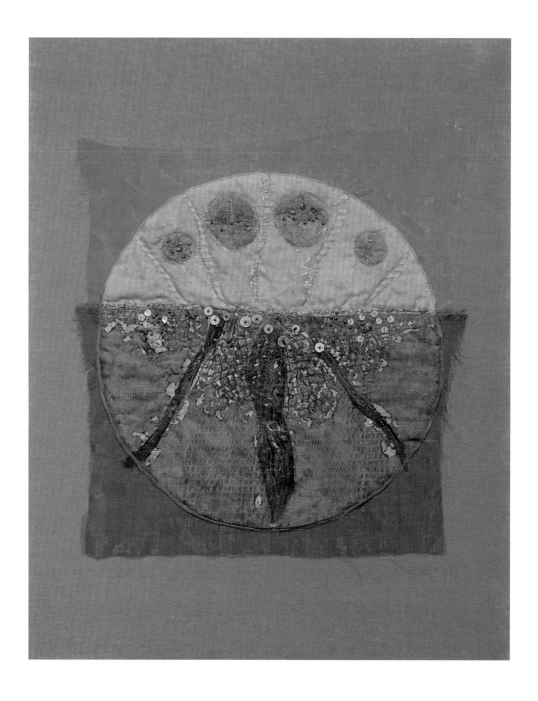

7701 Normandy Blvd.
Indianapolis, Indiana 46278 USA
317-872-2424 • Cell: 317-432-1668
cmyers83@comcast.net
www.carollmyers.com

Shield Series: Transformation
© 2008
32" x 24"
81 x 61 cm

# Ree Nancarrow

Photo: Eric Nancarrow

Mountains With Willows
© 2009
32" x 30"
81 x 76 cm

P.O. Box 29
Denali National Park, Alaska  99755  USA
907-683-2376
reenan@mtaonline.net

# Dominie Nash

8612 Rayburn Road
Bethesda, Maryland  20817  USA
202-722-1407
dominien@verizon.net
www.dominienash.com

Stills From a Life 34
© 2008
40" x 60"
102 x 152 cm

# Sylvia Naylor

Sunset | 49 Scrimger Avenue
© 2009 | Cambridge, Ontario  N1R 4V9
17" x 24" | Canada
43 x 61 cm | 519-620-4503
sylvia.naylor@sympatico.ca
www.sylvianaylor.com

# Jean Neblett

Photo: Sibila Savage

628 Rhode Island Street
San Francisco, California  94107  USA
415-550-2613  •  Fax: 415-821-2772
jeanneblett@gmail.com

Reflections 22: Sharon Woods In Winter
© 2007
35" x 40"
89 x 102 cm

# Stephanie Nordlin

PCubed: Prime.Primary.Primordial
© 2008
42" x 42"
107 x 107 cm

1672 Candlewick Drive S.W.
Poplar Grove, Illinois  61065  USA
815-765-0498  •  Cell: 815-260-0307
snfashiony@yahoo.com
www.stephanienordlin.com

# Maureen O'Doogan

1920 Longview Drive
Tallahassee, Florida 32303 USA
850-251-6605
MaureenODoogan@aol.com
www.MaureenODoogan.com

Me and the Pelican
© 2008
48" x 48"
122 x 122 cm

# Sonja Ohlmann

Photo: Sundal Studios

Inuit Antiquity
© 2007
48" x 76"
122 x 193 cm

R.R. 2
Leduc, Alberta  T9E 2X2
Canada
780-986-3746
sonja@sonjaohlmann.com
www.SonjaOhlmann.com

# Dan Olfe

P.O. Box 2106 | Cylinder Reflections #2
Julian, California  92036  USA | © 2008
760-765-3219 | 52" x 51"
danolfe@hotmail.com | 132 x 130 cm
www.danolfe.com |

# Pat Owoc

Photo: Casey Rae

Home Fires Burning
© 2008
48" x 79"
122 x 201 cm

816 Bricken Place
St. Louis, Missouri  63122  USA
314-821-7429
owocp@mindspring.com
www.patowoc.com

# Mary Pal

144 Broadway Avenue
Ottawa, Ontario  K1S 2V8
Canada
613-567-2675
marybpal@gmail.com
www.marypaldesigns.com

Waiting (Original Photo by Chalmers Butterfield)
© 2008
28" x 22"
71 x 56 cm

# BJ Parady

Strata 3
© 2008
37" x 22"
94 x 56 cm

1154 Wintergreen Terrace
Batavia, Illinois  62501  USA
630-326-9316
info@bjparady.com
www.bjparady.com

# Katie Pasquini Masopust

Photo: Carolyn Wright

235 Rancho Alegre Road
Santa Fe, New Mexico  87508  USA
505-471-2899 • Fax 505-471-6537
katiepm@aol.com
www.katiepm.com

Allegretto
© 2008
72" x 37"
183 x 94 cm

# Edna J. Patterson-Petty

Photo: Allied Photos of St. Louis, Mo.

Forty, Forty-Four
© 2009
35" x 35"
89 x 89 cm

3238 Lincoln Avenue
East St. Louis, Illinois 62204 USA
618-274-1878
ebonygirlp@aol.com
www.fabricswork.com

# Pat Pauly

2 Beech Road
Pittsford, New York 14534 USA
585-381-3921 • Fax: 585-381-3921
Ty610@aol.com
www.patpauly.com

Water, Earth II
© 2007
69" x 59"
175 x 150 cm

# Judy Coates Perez

Photo: Tom Van Eynde

Moon Garden
© 2008
56" x 69"
142 x 175 cm

1000 W. Washington Blvd., #505
Chicago, Illinois  60607  USA
312-829-1165
judycoatesperez@gmail.com
www.judycoatesperez.com

# Bonnie Peterson

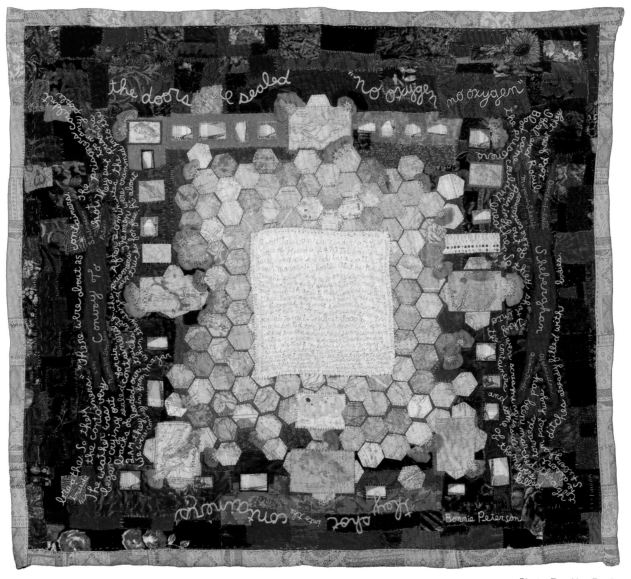

Photo: Tom Van Eynde

343 E. Ridge Avenue
Elmhurst, Illinois 60126 USA
630-673-5530
writebon@bonniepeterson.com
www.bonniepeterson.com

Convoy to Sheberghan
© 2007
50" x 56"
127 x 142 cm

# Mirjam Pet-Jacobs

When time goes fast
© 2008
33" x 30"
84 x 76 cm

Rossinilaan 9
NL - 5593 ZC Waalre
The Netherlands
+31 40 2217983
mirjam@mirjampetjacobs.nl
www.mirjampetjacobs.nl

# Julia E. Pfaff

Photo: Taylor Dabney

3104 Porter Street
Richmond, Virginia  23225  USA
804-232-3966
jepfaff@aol.com

My Week in Key Largo
© 2008
24" x 43"
61 x 109 cm

# Pixeladies
# Deb Cashatt & Kris Sazaki

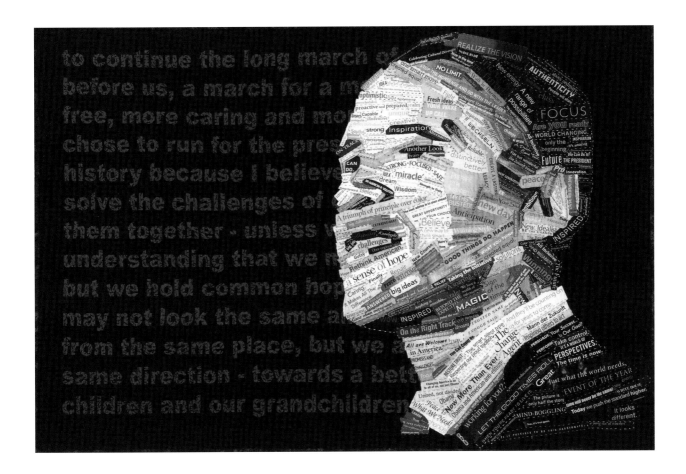

The Picture is Only Half the Story
© 2009
28" x 41"
71 x 104 cm

4061 Flying C Road
Cameron Park, California  95682  USA
916-320-8774
info@pixeladies.com
www.pixeladies.com

213

# Judith Plotner

Photo: Stan Plotner

214 Goat Farm Road | Iraq 2008
Gloversville, New York  12078  USA | © 2008
518-725-3222 | 43" x 60"
judith@judithplotner.com | 109 x 152 cm
www.judithplotner.com

# Clare Plug

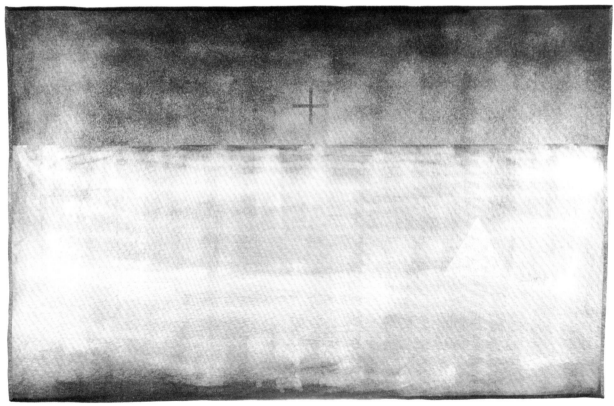

Photo: David Evans

Antarctica Series: Out on The Barrier | 5 Fleming Crescent
© 2008 | Maraenui, Napier 4110
47" x 72" | New Zealand
119 x 183 cm | +64 6 8437806
| plugac@paradise.net.nz
| www.clareplug.vc.net.nz

# Susan V. Polansky

Photo: Clements and Howcroft Photography

353 Mt. Vernon Street
Dedham, Massachusetts 02026 USA
781-329-6962 • Cell: 781-864-7197
harisue@comcast.net
www.susanpolansky.com

Pastoral Disturbance
© 2008
44" x 52"
112 x 132 cm

# Elizabeth Poole

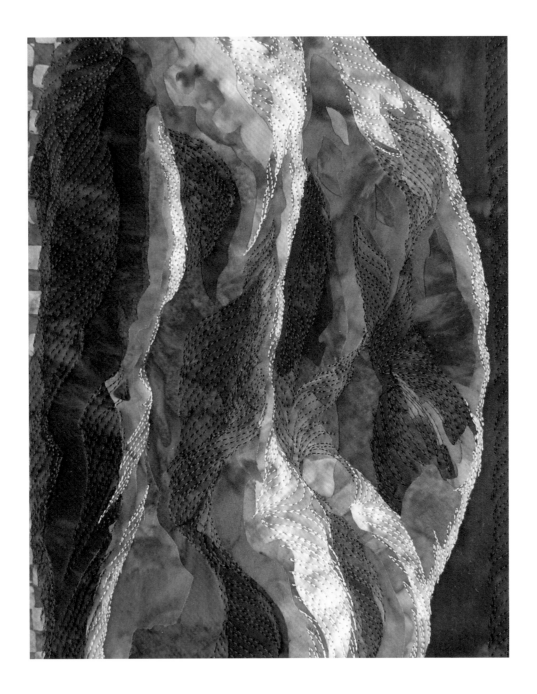

Study in Aubergines
© 2007
12" x 9"
30 x 23 cm

404 Old West Point Road West
Garrison, New York  10524  USA
914-482-0618 • Cell: 845-424-3136
elizabeth.poole@gmail.com
www.elizabethpoole.com

# Yvonne Porcella

Photo: David Lutz

3619 Shoemake Avenue
Modesto, California  95358  USA
209-524-1134
yporcella@yahoo.com
www.yvonneporcella.com

Dick & Jane
© 2007
66" x 78"
168 x 198 cm

# Casey Puetz

Photo: William Lemke

Serenity
© 2008
20" x 14"
51 x 36 cm

515 South Grandview Blvd.
Waukesha, Wisconsin 53188 USA
262-549-0763
ppuetz@wi.rr.com
www.caseypuetz.com

# Elaine Quehl

1974 Gardenway Drive
Ottawa, Ontario  K4A 3A2
Canada
613-824-8050
equehl@hotmail.com
www.equarelle.ca

Losses 2
© 2009
45" x 45"
114 x 114 cm

# Wen Redmond

Trees Seen, Forest Remembered
© 2008
24" x 33"
61 x 84 cm

First Star Farm
441 First Crown Point Road
Strafford, New Hampshire  03884  USA
603-332-8478
wenreddy@yahoo.com
www.WenRedmond.com

# Leslie Rego

Photo: F. Alfredo Rego

P.O. Box 2358
Sun Valley, Idaho  83353  USA
quilt@LeslieRego.com
www.LeslieRego.com

Sudden Gale
© 2008
27" x 20"
69 x 51 cm

# Sue Reno

Big Root Geranium
© 2008
38" x 43"
97 x 109 cm

3824 Hillcrest Drive
Columbia, Pennsylvania  17512  USA
717-371-0061
sue@suereno.com
www.suereno.com

# Jan Rickman

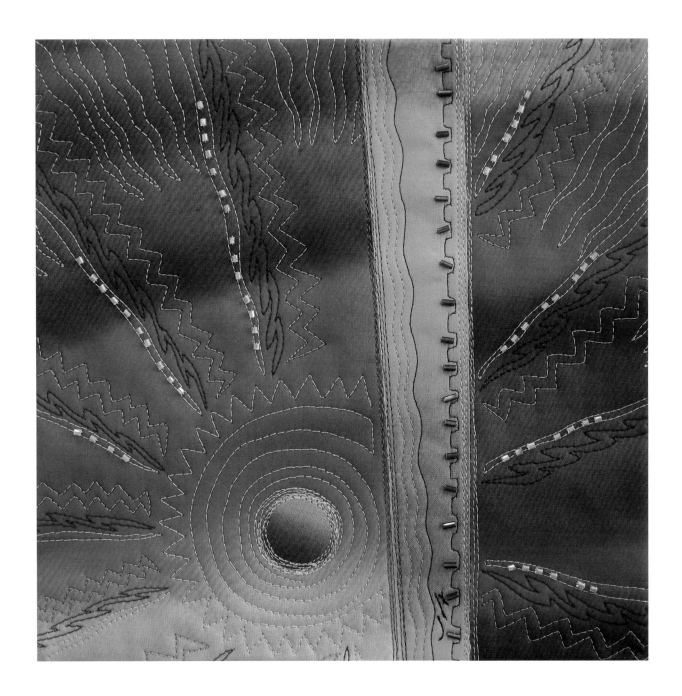

18303 Highway 141
Whitewater, Colorado  81527  USA
970-931-2231 • Cell: 970-201-0004
janfantastic01@yahoo.com
www.janrickman.com

Dream's Edge
© 2009
9" x 9"
23 x 23 cm

# Cindy Rinne

Photo: Steve Scudder

Stream
© 2008
19" x 21"
48 x 53 cm

P.O. Box 30261
San Bernardino, California  92413  USA
909-883-4005
cindy@fiberverse.com
www.fiberverse.com

# Kim Ritter

Photo: Rick Wells

834 West 24th Street
Houston, Texas  77008  USA
832-385-8100
kim@kimritter.com
www.kimritter.com

Biological Clock
© 2008
20" x 15"
51 x 38 cm

# Connie Rohman

Proustian Memory
© 2008
54" x 81"
137 x 206 cm

1031 W. Avenue 37
Los Angeles, California 90065 USA
323-225-3321
crohman1@yahoo.com
www.connierohman.com

# Pam RuBert

St. Louis - Wish You Were Hair
© 2008
54" x 41"
137 x 104 cm

1841 E. Bergman Street
Springfield, Missouri 65802 USA
417-862-3760
pam@rubert.com
www.pamrubert.com

# Rose Rushbrooke

6409 N. Orleans Avenue
Tampa, Florida  33604  USA
813-335-1634
rose@roserushbrooke.com
www.roserushbrooke.com

Woman
© 2007
30" x 20"
76 x 51 cm

# Carol Schepps

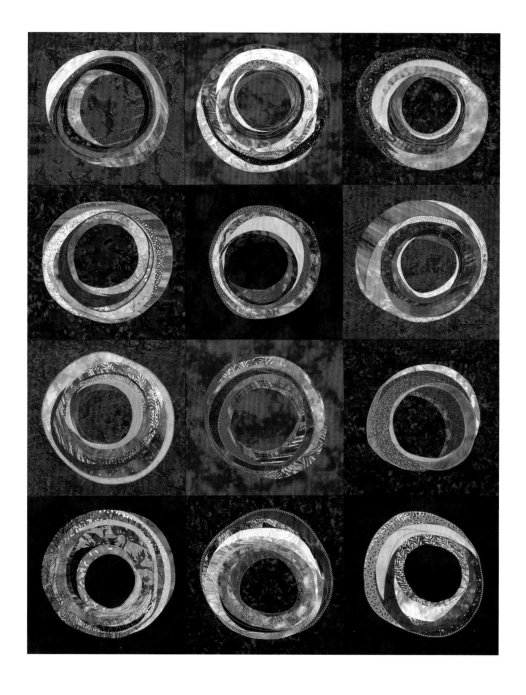

10 Marblehead Drive
Princeton Junction, New Jersey 08550 USA
609-275-9440
carol@carolschepps.com
www.carolschepps.com

Crescents 1
© 2007
52" x 39"
132 x 99 cm

# Norma Schlager

134 Logging Trail Road
Danbury, Connecticut  06811  USA
203-798-0025
nschlager11@comcast.net
www.NormaSchlager.com

Ocean Treasures
© 2009
48" x 28"
122 x 71 cm

# Maya Schonenberger

Photo: Werner Boeglin

Rejections | 8801 N.W. 189 Terrace
© 2008 | Miami, Florida  33018  USA
20" x 20" | 305-829-7609
51 x 51 cm | maya.schonenberger@gmail.com
| www.mayaschonenberger.com

# Karen Schulz

9204 Second Avenue
Silver Spring, Maryland  20910  USA
301-588-0427
campbellk@starpower.net
www.clothandchocolate.net/karen.htm

View
© 2008
70" x 42"
178 x 107 cm

# Alison Schwabe

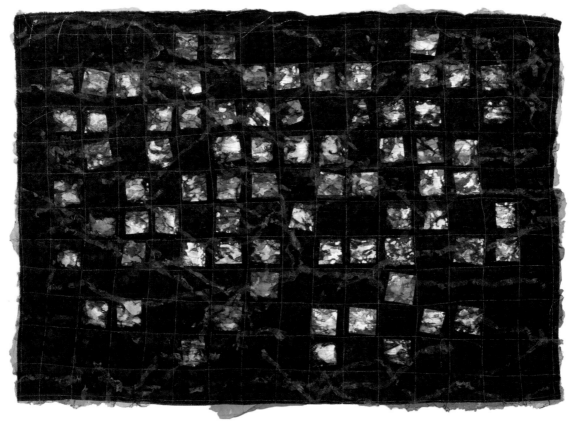

Photo: Eduardo Baldizan

Timetracks 9
© 2008
33" x 44"
84 x 112 cm

Divina Comedia 2041
11500 Carrasco, Montevideo
Uruguay
+ 598 2600 0053
alison@alisonschwabe.com
www.alisonschwabe.com

# Jayne Willoughby Scott

203 Rhatigan Road West
Edmonton, Alberta  T6R 1A2
Canada
780-437-7367
jscott@incentre.net
www.jaynewilloughbyscott.com

Waiting
© 2008
45" x 33"
114 x 84 cm

# Emmie Seaman

Three Wishes
© 2008
15" x 12"
38 x 30 cm

14900 North Orleans Trail
Stockton, Missouri  65785  USA
417-276-7794
eseaman@windstream.net
www.emmieseaman.com

# Merle Axelrad Serlin

Photo: Conor Collins and Maizie Gilbert

2600 14th Street
Sacramento, California 95818 USA
916-442-0464 • Fax: 916-446-0791
merle@AxelradArt.com
www.AxelradArt.com

Coast
© 2008
30" x 45"
76 x 114 cm

# Catherine Shanahan

Photo: Sharon Risedorph

Slice of the Cosmos IV
© 2008
46" x 35"
117 x 89 cm

5 Deer Path Drive
Portola Valley, California  94028  USA
650-851-9346
cathyshanahan@yahoo.com

# Kathleen Sharp

Photo: Wilson Graham

37640 Desert Sun Drive
Tucson, Arizona  85739  USA
520-825-8274  •  Fax: 520-825-8274
katsharp@sharpworks.com
www.sharpworks.com/studio

Goat in Boat
© 2009
48" x 45"
122 x 114 cm

# Carole Lyles Shaw

Letters Tell Secrets #1 | 5430 Lynx Lane #337
© 2008 | Columbia, Maryland  21044  USA
42" x 40" | 410-913-8539
107 x 102 cm | carole@lyles.net
| www.CaroleLylesShaw.com

# Sandra Sider

3811 Orloff Avenue
Bronx, New York  10463  USA
718-390-7473 • Fax: 347-602-6365
sandrasider@mac.com
www.sandrasider.com

Sea to Shining Sea: Arizona
© 2009
28" x 28"
71 x 71 cm

# Louise Silk

Raw Quilt #5: With All My Heart
© 2008
66" x 46"
168 x 117 cm

2250 Mary Street #201
Pittsburgh, Pennsylvania  15203  USA
412-431-2123
louise@silkquilt.com
www.silkquilt.com

# Valentyna Roenko Simpson

1048 Shafer Street
Oceanside, California 92054 USA
760-433-4808
valya@cox.net
www.royenkoart.com

The Ancient Beginning of a New World
© 2007
42" x 66"
107 x 168 cm

# Bonnie J. Smith

Photo: Gregory Case

Mom and Me          45 Devine Street
© 2009          San Jose, California  95110  USA
44" x 48"          408-298-7898
112 x 122 cm          bjs8934@aol.com
www.bonniejofiberarts.com

# Lura Schwarz Smith

Photo: Kerby C. Smith

P.O. Box 649
Coarsegold, California  93614  USA
559-683-6899 • Fax: 559-683-3061
lura@lura-art.com
www.lura-art.com

Stone Dreams
© 2009
41" x 22"
104 x 56 cm

# Mary Ruth Smith

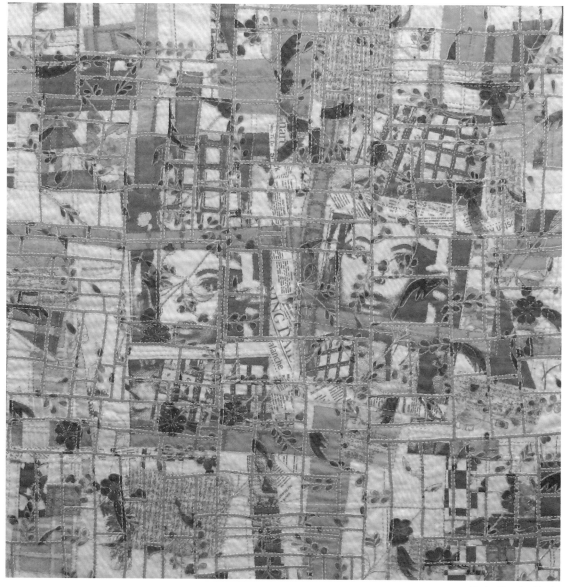

Photo: Sondra Brady

Avalanche Twins
© 2009
35" x 34"
89 x 86 cm

3400 Lyle Avenue
Waco, Texas  76708  USA
254-296-9495 • Fax: 254-710-1566
Mary_Ruth_Smith@baylor.edu
www.baylor.edu/art

# Sarah Ann Smith

17 Pleasant Ridge Drive
Camden, Maine  04843  USA
207-236-6003
sarah@sarahannsmith.com
www.sarahannsmith.com

Koi
© 2007
57" x 41"
145 x 104 cm

# Susan R. Sorrell

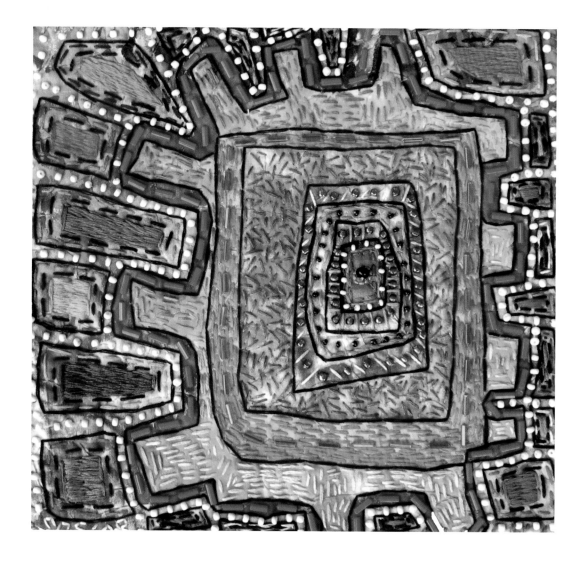

Let's make a Deal
© 2008
8" x 7"
20 x 18 cm

601 Cleveland Street, 12F
Greenville, South Carolina  29601  USA
864-517-4023
sorrell@creativechick.com
www.creativechick.com

# Cyndi Zacheis Souder

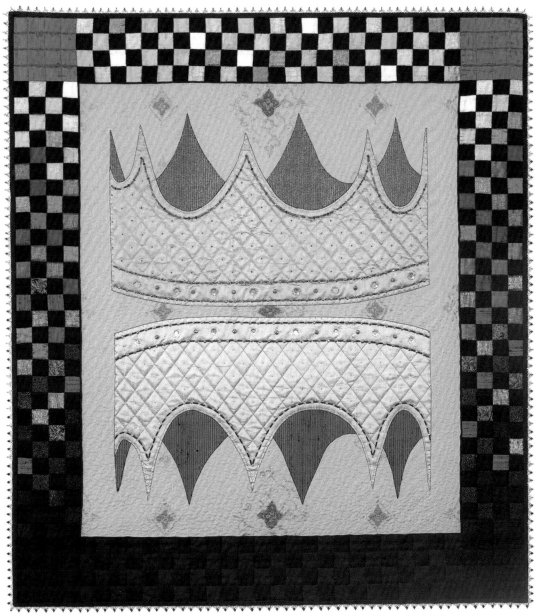

Photo: Thom Goertel

4407 Ossian Hall Lane
Annandale, Virginia 22003 USA
703-978-1357 • Fax: 703-978-1358
Cyndi@MoonlightingQuilts.com
www.MoonlightingQuilts.com

MonarchChromatic
© 2007
36" x 32"
91 x 81 cm

# Joanell Sowada

Photo: David Nicholas

City Mojo          206 W. Hogeye Drive
© 2008          Gillette, Wyoming  82716  USA
30" x 47"          307-682-1657
76 x 119 cm          jsowada@vcn.com
www.avacenter.org

# Marialuisa Sponga

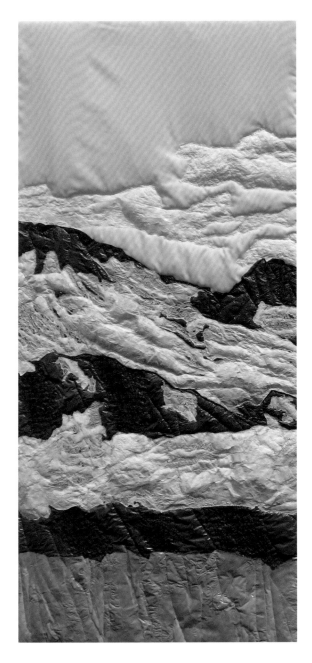

Photo: Giancarlo Sponga

Località Olgiasca, n. 60
I-23823 Colico (Lecco)
Italy
0039 (0)341 931 932
gisponga@tin.it
www.sponga.com

Clouds From Indoors
© 2008
60" x 57"
152 x 144 cm

# Teri Donovan Springer

There's One In Every Crowd
© 2009
42" x 34"
107 x 86 cm

120 Duke Street, Box 739
Chester, Nova Scotia B0J 1J0
Canada
269-615-6591
teri@fiberandthread.com
www.snowmoonstudio.com

# Sue Spurlock

1458 E. Gary Drive
Carbondale, Illinois  62902  USA
618-529-3080
suespurlock@gmail.com

Mother Pray For Us
© 2008
15" x 15"
38 x 38 cm

# Janet Steadman

Photo: Frank Ross

Night Fright | 2426 James Place, #303
© 2008 | Langley, Washington  98260  USA
53" x 56" | 360-321-0514
135 x 142 cm | jandon@whidbey.com
| www2.whidbey.net/jandon/

# Diane Steffen

125 Grandview Drive
Lake Ozark, Missouri  65049  USA
573-365-6422
dstef00@yahoo.com
www.dianesteffenartquilts.com

If I Could Fly
© 2009
57" x 32"
145 x 81 cm

# Tracy McCabe Stewart

Herons
© 2008
40" x 60"
102 x 152 cm

251 Parker Drive
Grayslake, Illinois 60030 USA
847-223-7032
tracy@mccabestewart.com
www.tracymccabestewart.com

# Julie Zaccone Stiller

1251 Highland Drive
Boulder Creek, California 95006 USA
831-338-4831
juliezs@yahoo.com
www.jzs.homestead.com

Spiral Recycles 4
© 2008
31" x 22"
79 x 56 cm

# Priscilla Stultz

Threaded | 3516 Cornell Road
© 2008 | Fairfax, Virginia  22030  USA
23" x 23" | 703-591-5630
58 x 58 cm | quilter73@hotmail.com
| www.priscillastultz.com

# Bobbie Sullivan

382 Hatherly Road
Scituate, Massachusetts 02066 USA
781-545-4867
bobbie382@comcast.net
www.bobbiesullivan.com

Crescent Lake View
© 2008
22" x 19"
56 x 48 cm

# Mary Will Sussman

Urban Avalanche
© 2007
26" x 32" x 3"
66 x 81 x 8 cm

1482 Pleasant Street
Webster, New Hampshire  03303  USA
603-648-2595
mews@websterridge.com
www.marywillsussman.com

# Sylvia Sutherland

Photo: Sharon Risedorph

344 View Street
Mountain View, California 94041 USA
650-390-9700
sylviasu@pacbell.net

Desert Valley
© 2008
34" x 46"
86 x 117 cm

# Mary Tabar

Photo: Jack Yonn

17616 Matinal Drive
San Diego, California 92127 USA
858-592-8828
piecing@hotmail.com
www.marytabar.com

Fiber Existence
© 2007
34" x 46"
86 x 117 cm

# Tiziana Tateo

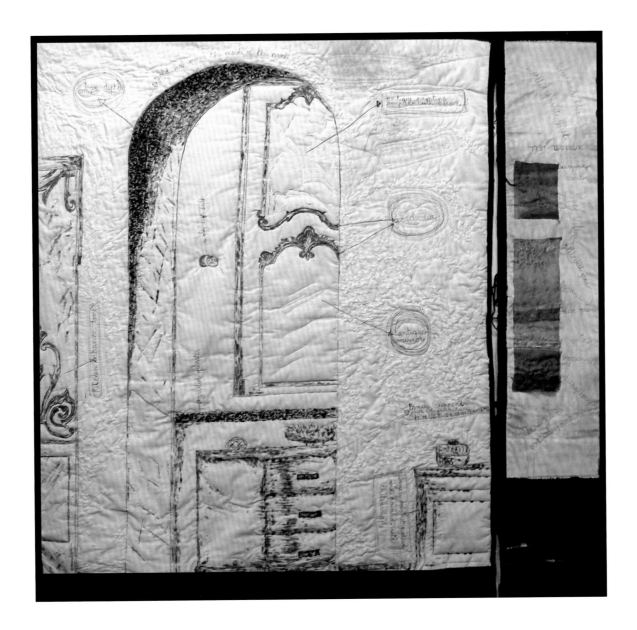

Beyond the Arch
© 2007
47" x 48"
119 x 122 cm

via Fratelli Cagnoni, 12
27029 Vigevano
Italy
+39 0381 690617 • Fax: +39 0381 70797
vtateo@alice.it
www.tizianatateo.it

# Carol Taylor

234 Railroad Mills Road
Pittsford, New York  14534  USA
585-381-4425
ctquilts@rochester.rr.com
www.caroltaylorquilts.com

September Song
© 2008
72" x 62"
183 x 158 cm

# Daphne Taylor

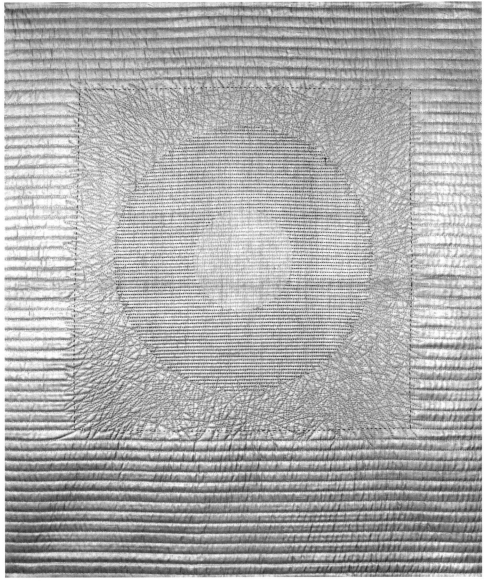

Photo: Karen Bell

Quilt Drawing #10 | 40 Harrison Street, Apt. 34E
© 2008 | New York, New York  10013  USA
43" x 36" | 212-240-0281 • Fax: 917-843-2446
109 x 91 cm | daphnetaylorquilts@gmail.com
www.daphnetaylorquilts.com

# Kate Themel

49 Briar Court
Cheshire, Connecticut  06410  USA
203-272-6171
kate123@cox.net
www.katethemel.com

Ice Water
© 2008
22" x 17"
56 x 43 cm

# Joan Potter Thomas

Deconstruction
© 2008
24" x 36"
61 x 91 cm

20643 Lexington Court
Northville, Michigan  48167  USA
248-449-4237
ajzbathomas@peoplepc.com
www.joanpotterthomas.com

# Gwyned Trefethen

Photo: Joe Ofria

223 S. Main Street
Sherborn, Massachusetts 01770 USA
gwynedtrefethen@mac.com
www.gwynedtrefethen.com

Entwined
© 2008
64" x 48"
163 x 122 cm

# Janet Twinn

Lightwave Variation
© 2008
48" x 52"
122 x 132 cm

Woodfield
11a, Tower Road
Tadworth, Surrey  KT20 5QY
United Kingdom
+44 (0) 1737 812136
www.janettwinn.co.uk

# June Underwood

Photo: Bill Bachhuber

1405 S.E. Main Street
Portland, Oregon 97214-3644 USA
503-233-8071
june@juneunderwood.com
www.juneunderwood.com

Dusk at the High Note
© 2008
12" x 12"
30 x 30 cm

# Grietje van der Veen

On the Forest Track I
© 2008
30" x 28"
76 x 70 cm

Hohestrasse 134
CH-4104 Oberwil
Switzerland
+41(0)614015655
grietje@textileart.ch
www.textileart.ch

# Melitta VanderBrooke

108 Meadowview Drive
Newtown, Pennsylvania  18940  USA
215-321-8748
Melittavbk@comcast.net

Windfall
© 2007
32" x 35"
81 x 89 cm

# Mary Vaneecke

Photo: Ron McCoy Photography

Circles III
© 2008
59" x 42"
150 x 107 cm

El Sol Quilting Studio
2000 South Hermosa
Tucson, Arizona  85713  USA
520-444-7149
mary@maryvaneecke.com
www.maryvaneecke.com

# Desiree Vaughn

5900 S. Calle Court
Suttons Bay, Michigan  49682  USA
231-409-2581
desiree@desireevaughn.com
www.desireevaughn.com

Summer's End
© 2008
20" x 37"
51 x 94 cm

# Terry Waldron

The Edge of Morning
© 2009
48" x 36"
122 x 91 cm

6160 E. Morningview Drive
Anaheim, California 92807 USA
714-921-1143
terryannwaldron@earthlink.net
www.terrywaldron.com

# Lisa Walton

Photo: John Doughty

23 Fred Street
Lewisham, New South Wales  2049
Australia
61 2 95607625
info@dyedheaven.com
www.dyedheaven.com

Bushfire Sunset
(Made by Lisa Walton and Nic Bridges)
© 2008
80" x 80"
203 x 203 cm

# Nelda Warkentin

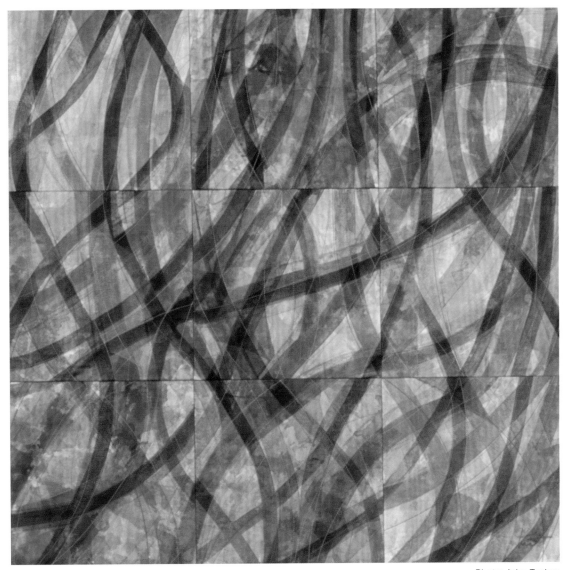

Photo: John Tuckey

Interlaced
© 2007
30" x 30"
76 x 76 cm

1130 West 6th Avenue, #7
Anchorage, Alaska 99501 USA
907-279-0907
nelda@acsalaska.net
www.neldawarkentin.com

# Laura Wasilowski

324 Vincent Place
Elgin, Illinois  60123  USA
847-931-7684
laura@artfabrik.com
www.artfabrik.com

Housing Department #7
© 2007
13" x 13"
33 x 33 cm

# Carol Watkins

Photo: Ken Sanville

Prairie Rainbow
© 2009
34" x 42"
86 x 107 cm

3702 Telluride Circle
Boulder, Colorado 80305 USA
303-494-5894
carol@carolwatkins..com
www.CarolWatkins.com

# Carol Ann Waugh

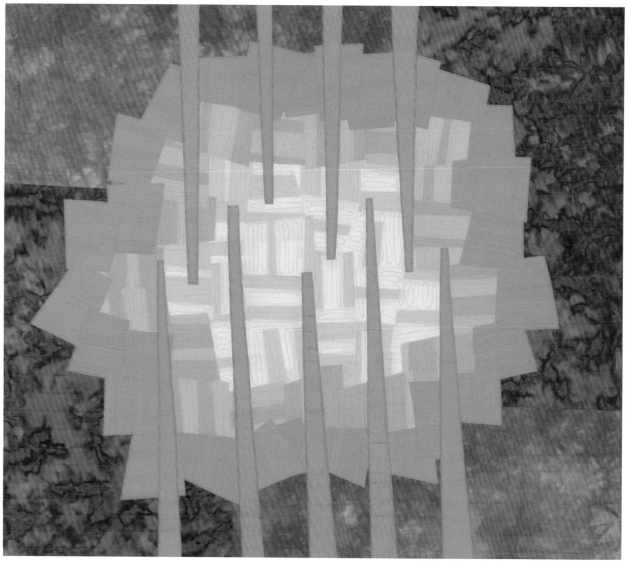

Photo: Marcia Ward

1163 Vine Street
Denver, Colorado 80206 USA
303-388-5215 • Fax: 303-388-0477
Carol@CarolAnnWaugh.com
www.CarolAnnWaugh.com

Yellow Submarine
© 2007
32" x 30"
81 x 76 cm

# Kathy Weaver

Photo: Tom Van Eynde

Generated Topology
© 2008
43" x 49"
109 x 124 cm

2713 Port Clinton Road
Highland Park, Illinois 60035 USA
847-432-0734
kweaverarts@comcast.net
www.kweaverarts.com

# Deborah Weir

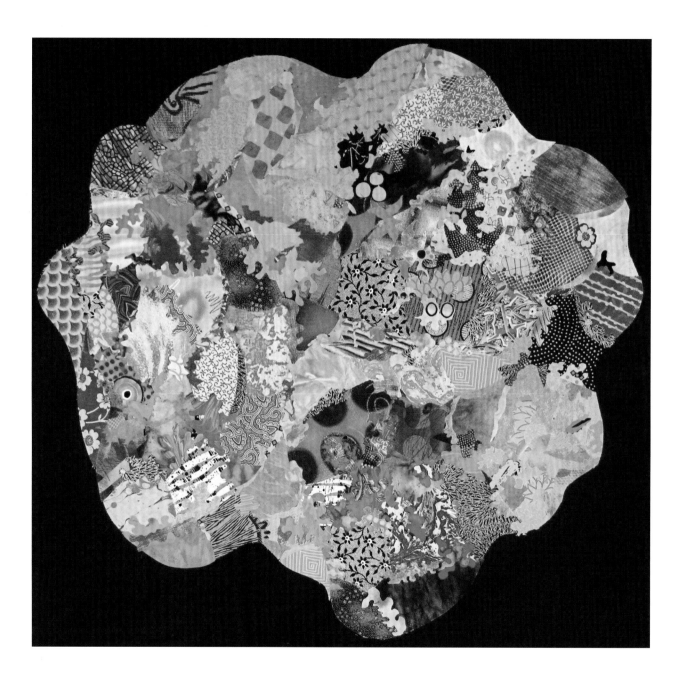

21 Encanto Drive
Rolling Hills Estates, California  90274  USA
310-325-1895
FiberFly@cox.net
www.DeborahWeir.net

Coalescence III
© 2008
27" x 28"
69 x 71 cm

# Sylvia Weir

La Mujer
© 2008
27" x 12"
68 x 30 cm

148 S. Dowlen Road, PMB 726
Beaumont, Texas 77707 USA
409-833-5217
weir_sm@hotmail.com
www.sylviaweir.com

# Maggie Weiss

2744 Lawndale Avenue
Evanston, Illinois  60201  USA
847-492-0204 • Cell: 847-571-1385
msmaggie6@comcast.net
www.maggieweiss.com

Canopy
© 2009
51" x 48"
129 x 122 cm

# Barbara J. West

Velvet Night
© 2009
14" x 23"
36 x 58 cm

1020 9th Avenue
Canmore, Alberta  T1W 1Z6
Canada
403-678-6500 • Fax: 403-668-5422
barbarajwest@nucleus.com

# Leni Levenson Wiener

Photo: Tim Grondin

321 Beechmont Drive
New Rochelle, New York  10804  USA
914-654-0366
Leni@leniwiener.com
www.leniwiener.com

Endless Dance of the Ponytail
© 2008
30" x 30"
76 x 76 cm

# Marianne R. Williamson

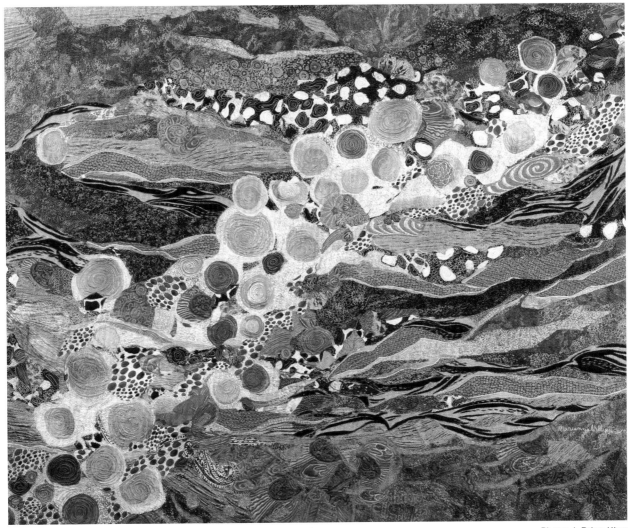

Photo: J. Brian King

Pebbles in the sand
© 2009
41" x 49"
104 x 124 cm

9300 S.W. 103 Street
Miami, Florida 33176 USA
505-429-6170
leapingdeerranch@gmail.com
www.movinthreads.com

# Sandra L.H. Woock

Photo: Mark Gulezian

5609 Greentree Road
Bethesda, Maryland 20817 USA
301-530-0035 • Cell: 303-789-8511
slhwoock@comcast.net
www.sandrawoock.com

Bang
© 2007
79" x 37"
201 x 94 cm

# Kathy York

Vertigo
© 2007
60" x 27"
152 x 69 cm

4202 Hyridge Drive
Austin, Texas 78759 USA
512-338-4271
kakiyork@gmail.com
www.aquamoonartquilts.blogspot.com

# Charlotte Ziebarth

3070 Ash Avenue
Boulder, Colorado 80305 USA
303-494-2601
cziebarth@aol.com
www.charlotteziebarth.com

Nine Moons: Sand Pictures #4
© 2008
42" x 34"
107 x 86 cm

# Artist Index

Virginia Abrams

# Artist Index

# Geographic Index

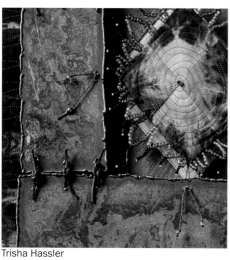
Trisha Hassler

# Geographic Index

Misik Kim

# Geographic Index

Alice Beasley

Studio Art Quilt Associates, Inc. is a non-profit organization whose mission is to promote the art quilt through education, exhibitions, professional development and documentation, Founded in 1989 by an initial group of 50 artists, SAQA members now number over 2,400: artists, teachers, collectors, gallery owners, museum curators and corporate sponsors. For more information on SAQA, please visit www.SAQA.com.